NEW DIRECTIONS FOR PHILANTHROPIC FUNDRAISING



Dwight F. Burlingame, Timothy L. Seiler,
Eugene R. Tempel
*Indiana University Center on Philanthropy*
EDITORS

# THE CHANGING WORLD OF FOUNDATION FUNDRAISING

## NEW CHALLENGES AND OPPORTUNITIES

Sandra A. Glass
*Philanthropy Advisor*
EDITOR

NUMBER 23, SPRING 1999

THE CHANGING WORLD OF FOUNDATION FUNDRAISING: NEW CHALLENGES AND OPPORTUNITIES
*Sandra A. Glass* (ed.)
New Directions for Philanthropic Fundraising, No. 23, Spring 1999
*Dwight F. Burlingame, Timothy L. Seiler, Eugene R. Tempel*, Editors



NEW DIRECTIONS FOR PHILANTHROPIC FUNDRAISING is indexed in Higher Education Abstracts and Philanthropic Index.

Microfilm copies of issues and articles are available in 16 mm and 35 mm, as well as microfiche in 105 mm, through University Microfilms Inc., 300 North Zeeb Road, Ann Arbor, Michigan 48106-1346.

ISSN 1072-172X ISBN 0-7879-4861-6

NEW DIRECTIONS FOR PHILANTHROPIC FUNDRAISING is part of The Jossey-Bass Nonprofit and Public Management Series and is published quarterly by Jossey-Bass Inc., Publishers, 350 Sansome Street, San Francisco, California 94104-1342.

SUBSCRIPTIONS cost $67.00 for individuals and $115.00 for institutions, agencies, and libraries. Prices subject to change. Refer to the Ordering Information page at the back of this issue.

EDITORIAL CORRESPONDENCE should be sent to the editor, Dwight F. Burlingame, Center on Philanthropy, Indiana University, 550 West North Street, Suite 301, Indianapolis, IN 46202-3162.

www.josseybass.com

Printed in the United States of America on acid-free recycled paper containing 100 percent recovered waste paper, of which at least 20 percent is postconsumer waste.

# Contents

Editor's Notes *1*
*Sandra A. Glass*

1. A new foundation for a new millennium *5*
*Dorothy S. Ridings*
As foundations' numbers and assets grow and they become more diverse, they must become aware of popular perceptions and must employ strategic planning to meet their new challenges.

2. The importance of focus in effective philanthropy *15*
*Hal Harvey*
Highly focused foundation programs can provide great philanthropic leverage if they include an explicit theory of change, employ peer review, and follow through on long-term commitments.

3. Regional foundations: Boundaries and opportunities *27*
*Neal O. Thorpe*
Foundations serving contiguous multistate areas are able to interact with regional agencies and to understand and serve the needs of their constituents.

4. Community foundations: Linking donors to communities *43*
*Alicia A. Philipp*
By bringing donors and community causes together to create effective matches, community foundations can have a positive impact on their local areas.

5. Building alliances for institutional support *51*
*Jeanne L. Narum*
When universities, foundations, and government agencies have a shared vision they can create partnerships to build and sustain high-quality programs.

6. Challenges of international grantmaking *69*
*Colin G. Campbell, Priscilla Lewis*
Foundations are broadening grantmaking in the post–Cold War era with increased support for economic, health, education, and environmental global issues.

7. Changing perspectives: Evolution not revolution *85*
*Sandra A. Glass*
Mutual understanding and frank communication between foundations and applicants can contribute to improved proposals, grantmaking, and institutional well-being.

Index *91*

# Editor's Notes

AS FOUNDATIONS PREPARE for the twenty-first century, they employ many of the same long-range planning exercises used by most nonprofit agencies. Indeed, many persons working in foundations today have come from nonprofit organizations. Yet their role as grantgivers, not grantseekers, adds a new dimension, and the purposes and inner workings of foundations may appear somewhat mysterious to prospective applicants.

Even experienced fundraisers, with great successes in obtaining individual or corporate gifts or bequests, often seem hesitant to approach foundations, and some have characterized foundation executives as "rich people in high-rise office buildings who arbitrarily throw bags of gold coins out the windows on rare occasions."

There are over forty thousand unique private foundations in the United States, with total assets of approximately $300 billion. As these foundations grow in number and size in the next generation, it is increasingly important for grantseekers to understand their missions and modes of operation.

Demystifying foundations is the focus of this issue.

Insights into what changes are taking place in different types of foundations can save applicants time and effort in applying to these donors and can encourage agencies to approach foundations to discuss priority needs that can have significant impact on communities, regions, and the nation.

The authors are experienced administrators and grantmakers who have perspectives on foundations that go beyond the bounds of their own organizations. Setting the national tone for foundation change in Chapter One, Dorothy S. Ridings identifies major trends that define new directions for organized philanthropy. The growth and diversity of giving will require strategic planning and continuing efforts to communicate foundations' roles to the public.

In Chapter Two, Hal Harvey asserts that focused or special-purpose philanthropy, with clearly enunciated goals, can be especially effective. Clarifying and testing processes, employing peer review, and following through on long-term commitments are essential if foundations want to accomplish significant change.

Using the M. J. Murdock Charitable Trust as an illustration, Neal O. Thorpe describes the thrust of regional foundations in Chapter Three. If they make an effort to know their regions well, foundations will understand priority issues and needs and will have special opportunities to support their constituencies.

Alicia A. Philipp, in Chapter Four, addresses the fundamental challenge of how to connect people in need with those who have the resources and desire to help. She describes how community foundations provide funding to needy recipients and serve both donors and grantseekers.

Jeanne L. Narum continues the themes of connection and cooperation in Chapter Five. The creation of public-private alliances, in which federal agencies and private foundations share goals and visions, will enable academic institutions to build programs that serve society creatively and effectively.

In Chapter Six, Colin G. Campbell and Priscilla Lewis describe the broadening of international funding in the post–Cold War world to include "human security" and "environmental security." These dimensions encompass the economic, social, and political aspects, as well as the military aspects of people's well-being and safety.

A number of foundations are beginning to collaborate with government and social agencies to address global problems and to increase Americans' awareness of international issues.

In the final chapter, I attempt to summarize the authors' ideas and to offer some practical suggestions on ways that grantseekers can improve relations with new and evolving foundations. Increasingly frank communication can lead to productive relationships and new areas of grantmaking that will benefit both recipients and donors.

The authors of this volume have illuminated the internal workings of foundations that many grantseekers do not see. It has been a privilege and pleasure to work with them.

Sandra A. Glass
*Editor*

SANDRA A. GLASS *is an independent consultant for education and philanthropy. She is program vice president emerita of the W. M. Keck Foundation, where she supervised higher education programs in science, engineering, and liberal arts for sixteen years. She also worked in development and administration for ten years at the Claremont Colleges.*

*The foundation of the future will differ significantly from the prototype of today, according to both informal data collection and formal research undertaken by the Council on Foundations.*

# 1

# A new foundation for a new millennium

*Dorothy S. Ridings*

SOMEONE WISE ONCE SAID that the only certain thing about the future is that it is not here yet.

True enough. But forecasting what the future is likely to bring is a vital exercise for almost any enterprise, including any foundation. And strategic planning based on that forecasting is clearly not just a trendy process; it is simply smart management and prudent stewardship.

For the Council on Foundations, forecasting and strategic planning are essential. Like many of our 1,750 member foundations and corporate giving programs, the Council has been engaged in developing a strategic plan that will serve us through the year 2004, and it has been a fascinating learning process. Much of it is necessarily based on assumptions about the nature of organized philanthropy in the new century, assumptions themselves based on both projections of hard data and educated opinions.

I was able to get an unintentional head start on harvesting those assumptions by simply arriving at the Council in 1996, without

NEW DIRECTIONS FOR PHILANTHROPIC FUNDRAISING, NO. 23, SPRING 1999 © JOSSEY-BASS PUBLISHERS

much involvement in the broader field of philanthropy beyond serving on two foundation boards and as an adviser or consultant to several others. It was clear to me that the Council's new president needed to know a whole lot more, firsthand, and the way to get that knowledge was to travel to meet our members, ask questions, and listen.

For two years I spent more than half of my time on the road, collecting information and ideas. Among the things I wanted to learn as I visited our members was where the practitioners in organized philanthropy think we are headed, as well as where we want to be headed—to get a handle on the foundation of the future envisioned by the field of philanthropy itself.

## *Trends in philanthropy*

Almost universally, I heard six trends mentioned:

- The field will continue its current explosion in numbers and assets.
- Grantmaking will become much more targeted.
- The field will become more professional.
- Accountability will be more important than ever.
- Competition will be ratcheted up.
- Diversity is the watchword of the future.

None of these even remotely constitutes a revelation, an "ah-ha." But taken together, they portend dramatic changes for all of organized philanthropy.

- *First, there is the issue of growth.*

This is a particularly important issue for the Council as a membership organization. I heard everywhere on my travels that the field would grow enormously, and nothing I have heard since then puts a damper on that prediction for the near future. Certain legislative and regulatory actions, such as the October 1998 passage of permanent status for the tax provision concerning gifts of appreciated property to private foundations, will only accelerate the trend, since many new private foundations are formed with gifts of appreciated stock.[1]

In fact, almost half of the 12,000 largest foundations in the United States have been created since 1980, according to the Foundation Center, and half of the 500-plus community foundations were established in the last decade. Council membership also is growing at a rate previously unequaled; by the end of October, about 260 foundations and corporate grantmakers had joined in 1998, compared with 158 new members in all of 1997—itself a record year.

Growth is continuing explosively in terms of assets as well. According to the Foundation Center, asset growth was strong during most of the twentieth century, with annual percentage growth in assets of the larger independent foundations hitting a high of 18 percent in 1996, the latest year for which complete data is available.[2] A continued strong stock market and the tax provision for gifts of appreciated stock to private foundations will undoubtedly encourage still greater asset growth; an informal Council survey in 1997 showed that the tax provision had clear and strong impact on both new foundation formation and additional gifts to existing foundations during the ten years the provision was in effect prior to its sunset in 1994.

The much-touted intergenerational transfer of wealth, in which an expected $10 trillion or more will change hands in the next twenty-five years from one generation to another, is another predictor of philanthropic growth. Many in organized philanthropy are working hard to see that some portion of those trillions goes into foundation giving.

- *Targeted grantmaking is already on the rise, and all indications are that the trend will accelerate in the coming years.*

Women's funds. Native American funds. Environmental funds. These and other specific interests are targets of funds increasingly being formed across the country, and practitioners of philanthropy expect that to continue. Annual reports are providing anecdotal evidence that today's new crop of donors, in particular, believe they can make a greater impact on a societal problem by "bundling" their dollars and focusing more narrowly on the avenues toward solutions.

Perhaps even more telling is the trend toward more targeted grantmaking in terms of the personal involvement of donors. The so-called new entrepreneurs of the baby-boom generation are interested in greater hands-on engagement with their grant recipients, a trend that is especially noteworthy to the charitable community that seeks volunteers along with dollars.

• *Professionalization of philanthropy is seen as necessary by some—and problematic by a few.*

Many different things can be meant by *professionalization.* Most of those who are promoting the idea talk about increased training for staff and trustees. Some are looking down the road at standards for staff certification.

The Council on Foundations has seen a marked rise in attendance at conferences and training opportunities, a rise that far exceeds the estimated 3.6 percent growth of the foundation field, the growth in our own membership, and growth in numbers of staff and trustees. There appears to be a real hunger for learning how to do things better, a sentiment we are hearing from conference evaluations and member surveys.

Further evidence of the trend comes from the growth and heightened activity of affinity groups, especially those of professional groupings such as the community foundations' associations for program officers, development workers, and financial staff. The number of affinity groups recognized by the Council on Foundations grew to thirty-six in 1998, with some of the most recently organized ones in the areas of grant evaluation, technology, and organizational effectiveness as opposed to the more traditional programmatic concerns such as education, health, and the arts.

• *The emphasis on accountability springs from both necessity and desire.*

If the entire nonprofit field has an Achilles heel, it clearly is accountability. Whatever the reality, numerous public opinion surveys show that the public believes this to be charities' weak spot.

Grantmakers, too, are inescapably concerned (even though Council research shows foundations' accountability ratings to be high), since the health and public approval of the organizations they fund are essential elements of effective philanthropy.

Recent legislative attempts at both federal and state levels aimed at forcing greater accountability show the dangers of not heeding this concern. The charitable sector has been largely successful at warding off egregious attacks that, rather than enhancing accountability, would hamstring important charitable activities such as advocating or even just participating in policymaking discussions with lawmakers. Grantmakers have confronted fewer direct attacks, although here too the threat is real, such as in current legislative attempts to restrict activities of corporate grantmakers.[3]

So the grantmaking world sees the real necessity for greater emphasis on accountability, as a way of strengthening public trust and fending off greater governmental oversight. Even more heartening, grantmakers are welcoming greater accountability, seeing it as an integral part of what philanthropy is all about.

Interestingly, Council research shows that Americans overwhelmingly believe foundations are accountable to the public, far more than to their boards, to regulatory authorities, or any other entity.

- *Competition is not exclusive to the for-profit sector.*

It never was. But recent times have accelerated attention to competitive pressures. Much has been written of the growing direct competition in the charitable world, as lines become blurred among the governmental, public, and private sectors. But in the grantmaking part of the nonprofit sector competition is heightened as well, most notably among community foundations. And few think the trend will do anything other than grow stronger.

A strong economy and increasing numbers of discretionary dollars fueled the latest wave of competition, in which various commercial enterprises—primarily financial management companies, brokerage firms, banks, and the like—have formed divisions to compete for charitable funds from individual donors. Commercial donor-directed funds are a direct challenge to community foundations in particular, and a war of sorts broke out in the late 1990s that will probably continue into the future, absent government intervention.

After some initial hand-wringing, community foundations got smart and began emphasizing their distinct competencies, those advantages that set them apart from the commercial firms. Stepped-up marketing has begun and will continue, based on the distinct features that community foundations can offer to make them the attractive choice for donors as vehicles for giving.

This story is far from over. The commercial donor-directed funds face a clear and appropriate challenge by the Internal Revenue Service as to whether they meet the requirements of the law, notably whether donors have too much control over how their gifts are directed and whether there is any "private benefit" (a real no-no) to such gifts. In the fall of 1998, a key staff member of the House Ways and Means Committee was suggesting that one solution might be to change the law so that private foundation rules would apply to donor-directed, or donor-advised, funds. The prevailing view in organized philanthropy is that the latter approach would be like using the proverbial elephant gun to kill a gnat (even though in this case, the pesky gnat is pretty big). Community foundations have operated donor-advised funds successfully for years without violating the laws governing public charities, and logic dictates that it is the commercial funds that need to be reined in.

Even without additional government regulation of donor-directed funds, however, my bet is on the community foundations. While it is not true of all donors, there is good evidence that community attachment, community involvement, is an enormous plus for those who do their organized giving through some vehicle other than a private foundation. And in that example, a well-managed community foundation in a donor's hometown has it all over the big bank in a distant metropolis.

More intriguing for the future-gazer is the competition we can not even foresee from entities we can not imagine. Those involved in U.S. foundation activity today believe there will be an increasing number of options for how donors do their philanthropy, options we do not even envision today, resulting in a lot more entrepreneurial thinking in the field.

- *Diversity and inclusiveness are vital descriptors of effective philanthropy of the year 2000 and beyond.*

The words *diversity* and *inclusiveness* sound shopworn in some ways, but there is absolutely no doubt that grantmaking will become more diverse and inclusive in both composition and practices. Dramatically changing demographics will drive much of that, as an even greater percentage of the American public becomes less like the original "barons of philanthropy" in terms of race, ethnicity, and other such descriptors. Wealth created in new venues provides another impetus; for example, there are now fourteen Native American tribes that have set up charitable funds (operating under tribal law that is separate from U.S. law, providing yet another challenge).

Still another major driver behind the changing face of philanthropy is the potential influx of new donors resulting from that intergenerational transfer of wealth, a trend we have already begun to realize. And an intriguing challenge to philanthropy is how to identify those new donors, both before and after the transfer takes place. These are donors who are not coming from positions of tremendous or traditional wealth. In fact, the current potential donors—the older generation of the two—may even be surprised to learn that their savings rates since World War II, their investments in homes that appreciated enormously, the growth of their investments after the advent of 401(k) and similar plans, and other factors have provided them the resources to think philanthropically rather than just charitably. And the potential heirs to whom much of this wealth is expected to be transferred need basic education in how the philanthropic impulse fits in with their other plans.

Adding to the changing picture is the growing globalization of philanthropy, which is diversifying the face of philanthropy in new ways. The Council has fifty-five members that are not U.S.-based, and we are increasingly contacted by philanthropists from other countries seeking to become more connected with organized philanthropy here.

The Council itself now has collegial agreements with nine grantmaking associations in other parts of the world—Australia, Brazil, Canada, Mexico, South Africa, Spain, New Zealand, the United Kingdom, and all of Europe. And a Council-sponsored conference for these and other colleague organizations in early 1997 was attended by twenty-one non-U.S. associations serving grantmakers. The Council's board of directors is talking seriously about the most helpful and appropriate ways for us to encourage philanthropic activity worldwide.

## *Survey research findings*

These expectations of philanthropy of the future, heard during my travels, are being confirmed daily as part of other, more formal research conducted by the Council. Some of it comes from our work on that 2000–2004 strategic plan, which will be completed by summer of 1999. Consultants to the Council have interviewed scores of people familiar with the philanthropic scene to gain insights that will guide us in our planning process.

And still other knowledge comes from research we commissioned as part of the Council's Communications/Legislative Initiative, a three-year project begun in 1997 in which we seek to convey a greater understanding of the value of philanthropy to legislators, the media, and other opinion leaders. The research shaping the project is based on 70 in-depth personal interviews with "influentials," 901 telephone surveys (half with "influentials" and half with the general public), interviews with 150 Fortune 1000 executives, and personal surveys of about 25 key Capitol Hill staff.

The research, released in December 1998, confirms some hunches and gives us new knowledge about people's understanding of philanthropy, foundations in particular. Our plans for how we will use the information to achieve the objectives of the initiative are still being set, but the findings themselves have other uses as well—including the forecasting of the future that is shaping our strategic plan.

Among the key findings:

- *Familiarity.* Although people are familiar with foundations, they have a very low awareness of what they are and what they do.
- *Foundations and other nonprofits.* There is little distinction in people's minds between foundations and nonprofit charities.
- *Communication gap.* Foundations speak internally in terms of assets and processes. But external audiences believe foundations should focus more on positive benefits and results, on success stories and innovation.
- *Information sources.* Respondents most often receive information about foundations from television and newspapers, with word of mouth from friends and representatives of foundations considered least likely sources of information. When asked what sources of information are deemed credible, however, respondents gave higher rank to representatives of foundations and friends.
- *Taxes.* A majority of people agree that "the tax code should provide incentives to encourage charitable giving, including giving to or setting up foundations."
- *Advocacy.* Most respondents agree that "foundations have the right to advocate, speak out, and promote public policy issues to the general public and lawmakers."
- *Accountability.* The general public believes that foundations are and should be most accountable to the public.

It is an intriguing picture of a not-well-understood sector that does not even speak of itself in terms that resonate with the public. It is a sector that is credible when it does speak, but that often leaves the speaking to other sources. It is a sector enjoying tax preferences that are approved by the public, a sector that also has public support for its involvement in public policy, and a sector that is seen as a public trust in terms of accountability.

When you lay that picture of foundations beside the foundation of the future envisioned by foundations themselves, it presents a daunting challenge. And a fascinating one.

For organized philanthropy, the new millennium may mean the beginning of a whole new era. The future is not here yet—but it is certainly on its way.

## Notes

1. A provision of the U.S. tax code known as 170(e)(5) was made a permanent part of the code in an omnibus appropriations bill that passed Congress in late October 1998. The provision allows full deductibility of gifts of appreciated stock to private foundations (full deductibility has always been available to community foundations, which are public charities). The provision had been in effect for private foundations from 1984 to 1994 and was subsequently reauthorized several times for limited periods, until permanency was achieved in the 1998 law. This was the top legislative priority of the Council on Foundations during that time.

2. Two of the 18 percentage points in 1996 asset growth derive from the David and Lucile Packard Foundation, which realized a massive infusion of assets from the estate of David Packard, who died that year. The Foundation Center points out that in contrast, in 1994, with the appreciated assets tax code rule expiring, assets grew less than 4 percent.

3. Rep. Paul Gillmor, R-OH, introduced two bills in the 105th Congress (1997–1998) dealing with corporate philanthropy. HR 945, which he abandoned, would have required corporate giving programs to allocate their giving according to the directions of their stockholders, proportional to their shareholdings. HR 944, later redrafted and expected to be reintroduced in the 106th Congress, calls for additional disclosure about corporate contributions to a degree considered burdensome and invasive by the Council. Included are such things as a provision requiring disclosure of a corporate executive's volunteer board involvement, and that of the executive's spouse, with any charity receiving such a contribution. The bill also would necessitate exhaustive listing of grant recipients beyond what is currently required by law—a chilling prospect for a retailer with hundreds of branches, for example, that typically allocates a relatively small amount of corporate giving dollars to each branch, which then has total discretion over the local giving. It is expected that Rep. Gillmor will hold hearings on his proposals in 1999, following release of a Securities and Exchange Commission report on the matter that was ordered in early 1998.

DOROTHY S. RIDINGS *has been president and CEO of the Council on Foundations since March 1996. Her career until then was in the newspaper business, as reporter (Charlotte, North Carolina), editor (Washington, D.C., and Louisville, Kentucky), and most recently publisher of Knight-Ridder's Bradenton Herald, in Florida. She resigned her board positions at both the Ford Foundation and Benton Foundation upon joining the Council.*

*Highly focused foundations and programs can offer great philanthropic leverage—but only if they are built to demanding standards.*

# 2

# The importance of focus in effective philanthropy

*Hal Harvey*

SUCCESS IN BUSINESS is evident in the bottom line: net profits will, over the long haul, mark an enterprise as a success or a failure. Philanthropy has no such simple measure, and as a consequence has a mixed and poorly understood record. One can find stellar—even world-changing—examples of philanthropy, but these are far outnumbered by good-hearted but relatively ineffectual gestures at charity. The lack of clear measures allows the field as a whole to drift along with little differentiation between the great and the merely good.

It is crucial to understand what makes the difference. A strong sense of what works in philanthropy can be used to build a very powerful program and avoid waste. That is good for the donor, good for society, and in keeping with the public trust placed in tax-sheltered foundations.

This chapter looks at one type of philanthropy that has been especially effective: focused or "special-purpose" philanthropy. Focused philanthropy has a very rich history. It has had, over the last century, a principal role in building university science, eradicating yellow

NEW DIRECTIONS FOR PHILANTHROPIC FUNDRAISING, NO. 23, SPRING 1999 © JOSSEY-BASS PUBLISHERS

fever, doubling global agricultural production, building civil rights laws, developing contraceptive technologies, and charting a path toward nuclear disarmament. This list is by no means complete, but even in such an abbreviated form, it conveys the potential power of philanthropy.

Still this splendid record hints at a parallel failure: very few of the nation's foundations have a record that features such examples of success. The greatest achievements can be attributed to a relative handful of foundations. The reason, I would argue, is that most foundations engage in what might be called *charity* as distinct from *philanthropy*, with markedly different consequences.

## *The Rockefeller legacy*

John D. Rockefeller Sr., together with his adviser Fredrick T. Gates, enunciated the first principles of focused philanthropy and created, in the early days of the Rockefeller Foundation, a record of success since unequaled. Rockefeller's puritan ethic and belief in work instilled the first principle: Target the root causes of a problem. In particular, he called on his trustees to "exclude individual charity and relief . . . and focus on problems that go to the root of individual or social ill-being and misery" (Rockefeller Foundation, 1999).

To this date, this restriction is perhaps the most important differentiating characteristic between philanthropy and charity. Philanthropy seeks to change conditions so that individuals can better their lives, or to solve other systemic problems; charity seeks to help individuals.

But the Rockefeller practice had further wisdom. As John D. Rockefeller's wealth grew in the late nineteenth century, he found his practice of tithing severely stressed. He was receiving thousands of appeals for help, and was unable to read, much less thoughtfully act on, them all. He began to work through intermediary institutions such as the American Baptist Home Mission Society (Chernow, 1998, p. 241), having them make decisions about allocation to local groups. Vast commitments to eradicate hookworm were made through the Rockefeller Sanitary Commission and the International Health Commission; similarly broad philanthropic strokes were made through the Rockefeller Institute for Medical Research and a whole string of medical universities. In education, the principle was expressed through the founding of the University of Chicago. Thus the second principle: make wholesale grants, not retail commitments.

Rockefeller pioneered the use of expert opinion in decision making. In his biography of Rockefeller, Ron Chernow argues that Rockefeller wanted to "reduce waste and duplication in the charitable sphere and deplored the lack of study behind much giving. 'Today the whole machinery of benevolence is conducted upon more or less haphazard principles'" (p. 314). Frustrated by claims and counterclaims, Rockefeller built up a cadre of trusted experts and used them to help design his philanthropy. Again from Chernow: "Like the family's other philanthropies, the Rockefeller Foundation was attuned to the optimistic, rational spirit of the Progressive era, and drew on its new class of technocrats" (p. 568).

These three principles are still sound guideposts, but experience in the field suggests several others that are also important. The remainder of this chapter examines further practices that characterize the best-focused philanthropy.

## *A clear goal*

The first element in focused philanthropy has to be a clearly enunciated goal with attendant thoughts about how to measure progress toward that goal. This may seem obvious, but it is nonetheless quite rare. Foundations often describe their focus in such sweeping but vague terms as "promoting public involvement in civic affairs" or "enhancing the human condition." A recent Web search turned up a foundation that "is committed to the support of all aspects of the creative process for a worldwide community of artists," and another that seeks to "inspire individuals to make responsible choices and take direct personal actions to achieve a peaceful and environmentally sustainable future." With such vaporous goals, it is impossible to know whether their work has succeeded or failed.

The Energy Foundation, of which I am president, is a special-purpose foundation established by four of America's largest foundations: the John D. and Catherine T. MacArthur Foundation, the Pew Charitable Trusts, the Rockefeller Foundation, and the Joyce Mertz-Gilmore Foundation. Their initial decision to devote significant funds to the Energy Foundation was in part made because they had in mind a very clear goal: "to increase energy efficiency and renewable energy as a path toward a sustainable energy future." Energy Foundation staff and the supporting foundations can measure each term, so we know how we are doing. A looser definition—"promoting sustainable energy" or "solving America's energy problem"—would not exact much information about how we are doing.

Compelling and useful goals cannot be shaped without thorough debate leading to clear choices. Using the Energy Foundation again as an example: in selecting our goal, we decided not to focus on documenting the environmental insults from excessive fossil fuel consumption, nor on promoting natural gas as a transition fuel, nor on resolving the bitter debates over nuclear power. These are all laudable and worthwhile pursuits; they might be part of a generic "energy program" at a large foundation. We are of course criticized by some for our narrow focus, but it is precisely that narrow definition that has allowed us success.

## *An explicit theory of change*

Foundations are relatively minor actors in the American economy. Their resources pale in comparison to the private sector, or to government. They cannot afford to act in many venues, and can rarely directly buy what they intend to pursue. For example, no foundation can pay to repair or reform any significant number of public schools, but one could choose to test new teaching methods, or change policy to encourage more charter schools, or stimulate the teaching profession through better training, or fund the development of new textbooks, or promote local control of schools.

There is a vast array of means of intervention that should be carefully combed before launching a grants program. Some strategies are bound to be more effective than others. Some strategies will fit within a foundation's budget or time horizons, while others will remain beyond reach. Some are practical next steps in a long evolution of change, while others require revolution. Perhaps the most effective plans may not be within the comfort range of a foundation's trustees or donors.

No theory of change is perfect, and some will fail spectacularly. But without an explicit theory, it is impossible to discover success or failure, and it is very difficult to evaluate competing grant applications. A good theory has several elements:

- *Know who must change, and consider their motivations.* Building a change strategy requires insight into institutional dynamics, status quo interests, political momentum and inertia, marketing, and (sometimes most important) the ancillary concerns of different actors.

At the inception of the Energy Foundation, we asked why technologies to reduce energy waste in buildings are routinely ignored by the private market even when their annual return on investment exceeds 50 percent. We felt we would have scant chance of building an effective change strategy if we could not understand why the market failed to make such sensible investments.

It turns out, for example, that the building industry is rife with market failure, and we could not develop a decent strategy without understanding that. Consider:

Architects are not rewarded or penalized for the energy performance of their buildings. Developers rarely own the buildings, and consequently care little about life-cycle costs. Building purchasers—be they commercial or residential—generally find it impossible to measure a building's energy performance, and even when those figures are available, such features (or demerits) are generally swamped by concerns over price, location, and amenity.

And the tenants of most buildings are renters, not owners. Renters generally cannot make capital investments in energy-saving devices, and landlords rarely pay energy bills. And no one in the building sector—architects, developers, builders, owners, or renters—likes taking risks over mundane items like air conditioners.

The result of this brew of motivations is a veritable collapse in rational energy decision making, with vastly wasteful practice as a result. This is actually an abbreviated list of problems, but it illustrates the complexity of building a good strategy for change. If we failed to appreciate the motivations of each of the building sector's principal actors, our strategy would fail.

• *Study other efforts.* We also found that many good efforts to transform the building sector have failed. Energy Foundation staff studied the history of intervention in the building industry and found a number of dismal results. Demonstration buildings set new marks for what is possible, but only steered a few percent of developers to better practices. Fannie Mae promoted energy-efficient mortgages, but these have had a relatively lackluster response. Energy rating systems have failed to generate a significant market signal. And so on. Each of these ideas reflected some theory of change. All were valuable, but none seemed to us to offer enough potential for marginal change with limited philanthropic dollars.

We ended up supporting the development and promulgation of advanced building codes. This strategy has met with great success, and will help in time to transform the character of the building industry. In fact, the broad consultation leading to the strategy has been part of its success, since the work requires extensive involvement from many parties in the building industry.

This process was complex and time-consuming, but it led to a clear plan, clear metrics for change, broad support from the industry and the NGOs engaged in the field, and an obvious method for its evaluation.

• *Every step must be credible.* The great Indian energy thinker, Amulya Reddy, described social change strategy as a stairstep, with a well-understood starting point, a clearly articulated goal, and each step in between explicitly mapped. He then added that if any step along the way was weak or impossible, the whole strategy was similarly weak or impossible.

This, too, is obvious but largely ignored. If a brilliant plan to reform schools has support of the teachers, is endorsed by the media, has been well tested, and is cost-effective, but still comes square up against the governor's philosophy, the plan is useless—or must at least wait for a change in the state administration. A thousand good ideas have died for lack of some critical step.

• *Defining each step in advance of setting a strategy is necessary to avoid missing steps along the path.* At the Energy Foundation, we use these tests in evaluating grant proposals. Has the applicant identified, by name or position, those who must change? Can he or she identify their motivations for changing, or for not? What pieces must fall into place for the strategy to succeed? Can they each be so coaxed?

It is surprising how many good ideas fail one or more of the tests. The grant applications are intelligent and passionate, but they do not always consider each step to success. And if funders hold grantees to these standards, their own strategies should surely reflect them as well.

## *Peer review*

The foundation world has little accountability. This is a great weakness. Few organizations will tell funders where they have erred for fear of losing support. In general, philanthropists are held in great esteem, not far from universal approbation: witness the term's prevalence in obituaries. This is all fine, but it does not make for a critical review. For any strategy to succeed, it must meet rigorous real-world tests. The best way to find out whether that is likely is to subject it to early criticism. Ideas should be gathered from many sources, and they should then be refined for vetting by real experts.

If a foundation is serious about building an explicit strategy, it should commit that strategy to paper—in draft form—and then ship it out for peer review. It should be critiqued by nonprofit groups in the field, by those who are the target for change (be they members of Congress, the media elite, scientists, or whoever), academics in the field, and other funders with similar programs.

The responses will not form a new consensus, but they almost inevitably help shape a stronger strategy. They also let those working in the field know of the considerations involved, and the process typically tends to build support for the new program.

The Energy Foundation holds regular strategy sessions focused on different topics. We invite experts to get together for a one- or two-day workshop, off the record, to critique current work and suggest new directions. We ask the group to lay out criteria for success and failure, to suggest high risk–high return outlier strategies, and to help think through different tactics in support of the work. These meetings include potential grantees, but also government agency directors, analysts, and industry leaders.

This process can of course be biased, and there is some danger of creating too many meetings for grantees, or in raising expectations about new program possibilities that do not come to fruition. Nonetheless, in shaping broad policy with long-term implications, there is no substitute for peer review.

## *Scale*

Focused philanthropy requires a careful matching of dollars to problems. Real progress in any significant issue requires large amounts of money. It might cost $100,000 per year for a decade to build a workable plan to protect a national forest in Colorado. For the Energy Foundation to be a serious player in building codes and appliance standards, we found we had to commit over $1 million per year. Global problems such as population control, climate change, or prevention of disease require tens of millions of dollars.

Most problems are tackled by several foundations, so partner contributions should be accounted for, but it is impossible to build and test any theory of change without a funding scale that relates to the problem. For smaller foundations, this may mean tackling a subset of a problem: change Bureau of Land Management grazing policies in Utah, build an AIDS prevention program in Hartford, curb sprawl in Reno. But whatever goal is chosen, it should be intelligently related to the funds available.

There is of course an alternative style of grantmaking, which is popular and appropriate for many foundations, and that is to give general support grants to several or many organizations working in a field. These foundations will not lead a field, but they are crucial for its health. This is not strategy-driven philanthropy, but it is still extremely valuable. When this choice is made, though, funders should be careful not to demand special contortions or special projects by the groups. The implicit strategy in field-building grants is that the field has its own intelligence and vector that should be supported.

## *Long-term commitment*

Significant change is rarely speedy. Institutions, cultural patterns, laws, and values all change slowly. Society's dampened responses no doubt save us from the perils of thousands of crazy schemes and zealots, but they also slow the acceptance of much-needed reforms.

Very few programs will be successful if they do not have staying power. Energy Foundation grantees could not successfully pursue clean energy plans in public utility commission hearings unless the groups can last past the initial skepticism, overcome roadblocks erected by utilities, build sound economic arguments, and muster political support. It would make no sense, then, for the Energy Foundation to support utility reform unless it was prepared to stay the course for many years.

The most successful foundation programs in history took decades to realize their potential. Even modern endeavors in philanthropy that seemed quixotic in early years are now proving their worth, but only because they have had time to unfold. The Ploughshares Fund, for example, has spent between $1 million and $2 million per year to reduce the threat of weapons of mass destruction. The fund's aims in the early 1980s—including a comprehensive test ban treaty, a new arms control treaty with the Soviet Union, a program for the control of fissile material, and regional treaties between potential nuclear nations—seemed hugely ambitious. But a constant aim and steady support gave Ploughshares Fund grantees the stability to work their agenda through many U.S. administrations, through different congressional committees, and through similar forums overseas. Today, many Ploughshares goals are mainstream policy.

### *Follow-through*

The parallel requirement to long-term support is follow-through. This requirement comes squarely up against the notion that foundations can forever seed new programs and then jump on to newer subjects. Seeding new programs is indeed exciting, but unless someone is around to water the seedlings, weed them, harvest the grain, and bake the bread, seeding itself is useless.

A brilliant scientific study on global warming means little if it has no media attention. Broad media coverage has marginal worth unless it helps spur new policy; that policy in turn is often ignored unless it is followed up with regulatory oversight and institutional change. And the whole cycle may need to be repeated to account for early policy design mistakes or further scientific information.

The foundation that is willing to stick with the idea from beginning to end can create lasting change. Those that only take on one part of the work, or only support it from year to year, are leaving their work to the whims of fate.

### *What this approach means to grantseekers*

Nonprofit groups seeking money plow through innumerable guidelines, looking for a match between their program and a foundation's interest. Many foundations have a field-building approach, and these are generally more ecumenical about targets and means of change. In approaching a special-purpose foundation, however, it behooves grantseekers to try to understand the foundation's underlying theory of change. Such theories should of course be made explicit in a foundation's guidelines—but when they are not, grantseekers should pose further questions.

If a foundation's programs seem misguided or missing an important element, grantseekers should by all means bring it to the program officer's attention. Peer review only works when peers are willing to review, and foundation staff should be prepared to defend sound thinking and modify the weak.

In my experience, the biggest failings in proposals are those that fail to articulate clearly a change strategy. Most proposals start with strong insight into a problem. Many go further to articulate a vision for a better future. But relatively few describe in detail how to change the situation—discussing in detail the actors, their motivations, and the steps to reform. This quality—understanding the means of change—is crucial for any social entrepreneur.

Conversely, nonprofit groups that can demonstrate their insight and proficiency in steering institutions to sounder practices have a relative cakewalk at the foundation door.

## *Conclusion*

The world's problems are far too serious—and philanthropic funds are far too limited—to tolerate sloppy or undisciplined approaches to change. This does not mean that experimentation should be avoided, or that field-building is not valuable: instead, it means that these and other approaches to philanthropy should be fitted into a disciplined, cohesive framework.

The essential tenets of a good social change strategy are few: explicitly describe the problem to be addressed, define the solution and be specific about it, name the people and the institutions that must be changed and discuss what is likely to change them, show how your program will accomplish change, and demonstrate the long-term commitment required for real change. Then subject the whole thing to peer review and clean it up as necessary. This approach will, more often than not, reap gratifying and even extraordinary rewards.

### *References*

Chernow, R. *Titan: The Life of John D. Rockefeller, Sr.* New York: Random House, 1998.

Rockefeller Foundation. [http://www.rockfound.org]. 1999.

HAL HARVEY *is president of the Energy Foundation in San Francisco.*

*Regional foundations face both special challenges and opportunities in the philanthropic world. If they take the requisite steps in coming to know their regions, they can offer their constituencies much more than signed checks.*

# 3

# Regional foundations: Boundaries and opportunities

*Neal O. Thorpe*

THE VAST MAJORITY of foundations are quite tightly geographically focused in their grantmaking, choosing to serve a constituency within an easy walk of the back porch. A minority have global, international, or at least national scope, sometimes spilling over a bit beyond our northern or southern borders. These foundations make grants well beyond the porch, often at distances not easily reached either by surface or by air.

In some zone between the back porch and our national borders resides the regional foundation. Its geographic territory is generally marked out, either defensibly or not, as some section of the country, less than the whole, but more than a single state.

## *Defining "regional foundation"*

Although a region can be thought of as any portion of the earth's surface, for our purposes we will confine our conversation to those foundations that serve subsections of the United States. Several dictionary definitions of *region* can be useful in characterizing the territory of a regional foundation, such as "an administrative area" or "an area containing a population whose members possess sufficient historical, cultural, economic, and social homogeneity to distinguish them from others or an area often with distinct natural boundaries." Often one or more of these factors are considered when a foundation determines the extent of its region.

But foundations, characteristically in the habit of making up their own minds about things, make up their own peculiar definitions of *region* as well. These may arise from historical idiosyncrasies or subject areas of interest or perceived needs or areas of corporate business, or almost anything else. A case in point is the foundation of which I am a part, the Murdock Trust, where the primary factor in drawing the lines around our region was to make it coincide with the territory of a Piper aircraft distributorship owned by Jack Murdock, our benefactor. While the lines were not precisely followed, this is a case where a for-profit region became a nonprofit region in which the for-profit organization no longer conducts business. It was probably done more to honor the hobby business interests of our benefactor than for any other single reason.

### *Foundation types and regionalism*

Some regional foundations have carved out discontinuous regions for their operations. This is not uncommon for corporate foundations, one of the four major foundation types. Corporate foundations tend to make grants wherever the parent for-profit has business establishments, and these are often scattered about the country. Since only about 5 percent of foundations are corporate foundations, and many of them grant locally, such scattered-region arrangements describe only a small fraction of all regional foundations.

A second type of foundation, the community foundation, is by definition *not* regional. Some make grants only in small, tight communities, while others may operate statewide. Only about 1 percent of all foundations are so classified, and because of their special roles they do not fit our multistate definition very well.

A third type of foundation is the operating foundation. Although operating foundations may be national or regional or otherwise, they make up another 5 percent of all foundations and most make few, if any, grants. Certainly some of these are legitimately regional grantmakers, but they are quite small in number.

The fourth and final type of foundation is the independent foundation. Independent foundations constitute about 89 percent of all foundations. It is not surprising that this group contains most of the regional foundations.

From what has been stated so far, it would appear that regional foundations are quite scarce. Unfortunately, their numbers are not well tracked and only estimates can be made of their occurrence. One gauge is to use our five-state region as an example. Of about 150 foundations that belong to a regional group of grantmakers, only eight are multistate grantmakers. Of these, two make grants in only two states and three in all five states plus British Columbia. To the degree this is representative of the nation, probably less than 5 percent of all foundations are regional foundations.

### *A working, practical definition*

It does not appear that regional foundations fit too well into a tight definition, but they have some characteristics that will allow at least a brief description. For our reflections, let us consider a regional foundation to be one that operates in a specific multistate geographic area, ideally contiguous, that is defined by one or more characteristics that enable the special interests of the foundation to be applied efficiently and effectively for the maximum benefit of its constituency.

It may be just as appropriate to say that a regional foundation is one that casts its net beyond the back porch, over one or more state lines.

## *Factors influencing philanthropic regionalism*

Most of what is discussed herein comes from personal experience with the Murdock Trust and from discussing these ideas with others. Murdock is a general-purpose regional foundation, covering five states of the Pacific Northwest, with an endowment of about $450 million and a staff of thirteen: four program directors, three finance and investment staff, five support staff, and an executive director. The Trust has a board of three trustees.

As indicated earlier, a region may be of almost any size. But whatever its size or characteristics, there are several factors that have a bearing on what foundations do in the region, how they do it, and how large a territory a foundation chooses for operations.

### *Asset levels*

The assets held by a foundation have a bearing on regionalism. There are well over forty thousand active grantmaking foundations in the United States. Only about twelve thousand foundations hold assets of $1 million or more, and only about six hundred hold assets of $50 million or more. Although no particular asset level is a requirement to operate regionally, it is difficult to be effective *and* regional at the lower end of this range. A small foundation may be able to handle a small region effectively, or a larger region with very narrowly defined interests, but these are few and far between. To be small and at the same time regional runs the risk of becoming a mile wide and an inch deep. In the foundation world, it is too easy to spread funds so thinly in response to needs that the region is hardly better off in any dimension.

Conversely, a high level of assets will not automatically cause or qualify a foundation to become regional in scope. Some of the very large foundations that have recently been created, including some as large as $1 billion in assets, have decided to operate within the borders of their own states, or parts of a state. It is not uncommon for this to occur for newly formed foundations where the belief is held that funds earned locally during the life of the benefactor should have local impact. If the foundation is large and its region small, it may find it impossible to meet the required payout by means of wise grantmaking and may have to resort to enlarging its geographic workplace.

We find our asset level at Murdock to be quite appropriate for our region, provided we adhere to our primary interests and do not dilute our efforts excessively by trying to meet every need to which we are exposed.

### *Grantmaking interests*

The grantmaking interests held by a foundation also have a bearing on regionalism. It is obvious that if a foundation is interested in supporting efforts to recover better levels of salmon returning upstream from the ocean, it would make sense to choose a region wherein this activity occurs rather than to operate remotely from some distant section of the country. If the interests are in solving problems related to urban decay, a region that contains several examples of this would be highly favored over one where there is little of this occurring. Many other examples could be given, all of which are commonsense approaches to determining the size, shape, and location of a region.

Other factors, such as terrain, the political climate, types of educational institution, economics, health care delivery, specific disease pockets, and so on, may all be important in determining whether or not a foundation should operate regionally rather than locally or nationally.

### *Knowing the region*

The factors mentioned thus far do not constitute an exhaustive list of possibilities affecting regionalism. But there is yet another that we at Murdock believe to be *the most important of all* in determining the legitimacy of a foundation viewing itself as regional and operating effectively as such. That factor is the degree to which a foundation "knows" its region. For well-informed and wise grantmaking, there is simply no substitute for knowing the region: its issues, needs, strengths, people, organizations, experts, leaders and followers, resources, and even other grantmakers. A foundation should not carve out a region of operation within which it cannot really know the territory well. Because of this, many wisely operate from the back porch, where the territory is more familiar.

## *Challenges of being a regional foundation*

Regional foundations have a number of special challenges that come with the territory. Most of them can be viewed as related to the acquisition of that important grantmaker's asset: knowing the region.

### *Three grantmaking styles*

A foundation's operational style will greatly influence how deeply it comes to know its region. Operationally speaking, and perhaps somewhat theoretically, a foundation can be thought of as one of three types: proactive, reactive, or interactive. *Proactive* foundations may view a region, see a set of problems, and propose a solution. Those who apply for support to address the problem in a way that fits the foundation, and have worthy approaches, are funded. A strictly proactive foundation, if such exists, would probably come to know a region from its own perspective, depending upon its in-house expertise and what it chooses to see in the region. There is no certainty that it will know its region very well.

*Reactive* foundations lie in wait for requests, evaluate them, and fund the best. These foundations are pretty much at the mercy of what comes in the door and know their regions only to that degree. If important projects present themselves for funding, the reactive foundation will indeed know about those that appear. But it may not know about other important efforts in the region that do not make an appearance for support but could be models against which a proposed project may be measured. Such a reactive style often leaves a foundation deprived of important information.

While it is clear that these two models are depicted as extremes, perhaps somewhat harshly, they do in fact exist to varying degrees in the foundation world. All foundations will probably fit on a continuum from one extreme to the other.

A middle ground approach that we at Murdock practice is to be interactive. The *interactive* approach is challenging but one we believe to be the best operational style to practice in gaining a thorough knowledge of the region.

### *Knowing a region by interactivity*

Interactive grantmaking begins by getting out into the region, listening, and learning. This requires staff of sufficient number and skill to cover the region well and with open-eared but objective attention. Thus, one of the great challenges of regionalism is a willingness of the foundation to staff up properly to cover the ground. If the interests of the foundation are extremely narrow, a small staff will do, while if the foundation is a general-purpose one, wider-ranging expertise is necessary. Our four program directors are out in the field a good percentage of their time, conducting site visits for virtually all pending proposals and meeting with organizations and people related to the subject areas in which we give grants. This high level of interactivity with the constituencies on their own turf is one way to meet the challenge of getting to know the region.

A second way to get to know a region, a good supplement to getting out there on foot, is to judiciously invite key representatives of organizations to meet together at the foundation offices. We do this often. As an example, since we support basic scientific research at graduate universities, we occasionally invite all chief administrative officers of research to discuss with us and with each other the special challenges they face in securing support. Two things typically happen when this is done. First, the foundation staff become educated on matters related to certain grantmaking subjects. Second, participants share ideas and insights that are of direct value to the participant group. As an important plus, all have an opportunity to get to know one another better. Meetings often lead us to develop and implement programs of support that meet critical needs. In general, this type of orientation enables the staff to handle all proposals from these institutions more intelligently. This mode of operation is a good example of interactive grantmaking.

Yet another way to come to know the region, perhaps more in the sense of issues than in the sense of organizations, is to invite persons of special expertise to help the foundation staff and board wrestle with issues related to the foundation's interests. We do this by inviting "visiting scholars" to spend a day or two with us, meeting with all the staff and board, concentrating on the program directors, and sharing ideas with a wider audience we select that may benefit directly from the visitor's expertise. For this activity we often prefer having someone come from outside the region who will bring to our table a national perspective, an important factor in keeping us from becoming too parochial in our view of issues. This approach, of course, takes time and costs money, but we have found it to be well worth the effort and expense.

Still another approach to learning about one's region, which we are using at Murdock, is to conduct studies of issues or organizations in the region. Since we expect program directors to be resource people with specialized knowledge of certain grantmaking subjects, this activity has the dual role of enhancing the program director's expertise and educating the foundation staff as a whole. As an example, we are currently engaged in a study of issues facing the people of Alaska, looking for opportunities to be more responsive within our subject areas of interest. We expect to come out of this study with a knowledge of how we can better serve this part of our region in the future, and the participants in the study will benefit by being well represented in our discussions and deliberations. Ultimately, knowing each other better should result in more efficient grantmaking and a better place for Alaskans of all ages to live.

### *Taking a clear view*

Hand in hand with knowing one's region is an ability to judge the region objectively. This means the regional foundation has the challenge of becoming familiar with or using national standards against which regional issues can be measured. A straightforward and often-practiced illustration of this is in the support of scientific research. Here at Murdock, proposals coming from regional universities are sent out for review by experts that may be in any part of the country. Hence, the research is evaluated by national standards. In other subject areas, program directors often do the same or, alternatively, expose themselves to issues of national scope and concern by attending conferences and workshops, and, of course, by having national experts come to the Trust to lend their insights to our local scene.

While our emphasis is on regional foundations, one example of a national foundation behaving like a regional foundation is worthy of note. The foundation in mind (the Research Corporation of Tucson, Arizona) supports basic scientific research in defined disciplines, requiring it to know institutions nationwide at which such research occurs. Wisely, for many years, the foundation divided the nation up into four regions, placed a regional director in each one, and depended on that director to be the most knowledgeable person in the whole region regarding the practice of basic scientific research. Indeed that was the case, and this foundation has no serious competition in terms of knowing its region, in this unusual case a territory of national scope. But note, it has reached this level of distinction largely because the nation was dealt with as a collection of regions, each of which was thoroughly known by the regional director.

Given these examples, it is apparent that getting to know a region has financial consequences for a foundation. First, there is a need to staff up to the point of being physically able to cover the region. Furthermore, the staff should have backgrounds that best enable them to understand and assimilate the information gained. Related to staffing are the cost consequences of travel, food, and lodging to thoroughly stalk the terrain. The more program directors necessary to do that, the more support staff required to back them up in a variety of ways.

Inviting in guests to discuss issues of concern to them requires staff to coordinate and make arrangements and a commitment to have facilities that allow it to happen. While these events are spearheaded by program directors, the support staff have important roles in creating an environment wherein the best and most productive discussions are held. We at Murdock are convinced that recruiting and nurturing a properly qualified staff of sufficient number is one of the best investments a foundation can make in its region.

Ideally then, a regional foundation should carve out a territory for itself in which it can come to know its constituency so well that wise and well-informed grantmaking can be conducted in the best interest of its people.

So why be a regional foundation? Basically, because the opportunities to serve the public good far outweigh the challenges intrinsic to being regional.

## *Advantages and opportunities of being a regional foundation*

While there are special challenges to being regional, there are advantages and opportunities that outstrip any of the negatives.

One advantage of being regional rather than local in scope is that the foundation staff are exposed to a greater variety of issues affecting the constituency, and more opportunities surface for grantmaking activities. Coupled with this is a greater availability of expertise, quite close at hand, for purposes of educating and providing advice to staff and board when needed on topics and proposals. Furthermore, the variety is stimulating to the grantmaker.

Another advantage is that knowledge is gained of several organizations with similar missions, such as groups of YMCAs or museums or sheltered workshops. This advantage provides the regional grantmaker with opportunities that rarely exist for the more localized foundation. It works like this. A program director, either in reviewing a proposal or in meeting with the staff of a grantseeking organization, may know of another organization that has addressed a particular issue in a creative and productive manner. Knowing both organizations as well as the issue common to both, the program director suggests the two make contact and gain from each other's perspective. This pairing of organizations, or sometimes gathering together several of similar ilk, is a highly productive and low-cost way of getting the best ideas on the table as well as a means to implement interorganizational education and problem solving. This will, of course, only be possible if the foundation knows its region well and can productively choose and bring organizations together.

Being regional rather than national, even when a subject area could be applied to the national scene, may allow a foundation to have greater impact. A clear example of this comes from Murdock's interest in strengthening faculty and undergraduate scientific research at private liberal arts colleges. With thirty of these in our region, we can be more responsive and provide more funding to each than if we were national and saddled with the task of understanding several hundred colleges. There are advantages in being smaller than national as well as in being larger than local.

## *The Pacific Northwest as a region*

Murdock's region is five states: Alaska, Idaho, Montana, Oregon, and Washington. Given the rationale by which this region was determined, we find ourselves with a territory that by land mass is discontinuous but by other measures has characteristics that allow it to serve well for regional operations.

It is a big region. Alaska alone makes it big, and Montana adds a large chunk of land. Were the region highly populated it would be too big for us, but within the five states there reside only about 11.5 million people, with 76 percent of these quite close at hand in two states, Oregon and Washington. Furthermore, the bulk of the population is clustered in only two metropolitan areas, Seattle and Portland. So from the point of view of population, we find the region to be a reasonable match for a foundation of our size.

Geographic discontinuity, although present, is not much of a problem. It is about as easy to go to the major cities in Alaska as to those in Montana, while both have isolated areas accessible only by bush plane or car. Barrow is about as easy to reach as Billings, so the size of the region is manageable given a resolve to face the costs of getting around.

Beyond population and geographic size, there are common-thread issues throughout the region. Certainly an obvious one is people's desire to live in an environment that still retains some pristine and frontier qualities in spite of the economy's historically depending heavily on natural resource industries such as timber, fishing, and mining. There are many moves afoot to work out balanced means of treating our land with economic approaches that are friendly to the habitat. These are issues that have great ramifications throughout the Pacific Northwest.

Our region is also a good one regarding the support of higher education and scientific research. These two arenas are major subject interests for us, with about two-thirds of all dollars ending up in support of both. In addition to the thirty private undergraduate colleges and universities mentioned earlier, there are about a dozen public research universities in the five states. Thus, although the region is large, the number of institutions is manageable from the perspective of knowing them well and making grants with a full knowledge of institutional strengths and weaknesses. Since the institutional density is quite low compared to other parts of the country, a foundation of even our size has the opportunity to know them well, be responsive to needs, and have impact.

Rural health care is another example of how parts of the region are tied together. First, there are only two medical schools in the region. One of these serves four states and the other a single state. This allows the support of medical research and training to focus on the area where the two main population centers of the region are located. The remaining territory is quite rural, raising the importance of rural health care delivery, which may require unconventional forms such as telemedicine and over-the-phone diagnosis. Finding a niche in rural health care means playing a role in a regionwide issue.

## *Opportunities beyond just grantmaking*

To say "just" grantmaking is not to belittle that activity, for grantmaking is the heart and soul of most foundations and certainly their raison d'être. But regional foundations, well grounded in the knowledge of the region, are unusually well situated and qualified to go beyond grantmaking in serving the public good. Over the years, we at Murdock have found several ways to strengthen our constituency, other than by grantmaking. We call these enrichment, or value-added, programs.

Here some examples are in order. Since one of our grantmaking areas of interest is health and human services, we interact with a group of widely diverse organizations. In so doing, we have come to know many nonprofits for which maintaining financial stability is a daunting task, sometimes so much so that it consumes time and energy to the point where the true work of the organization is marginalized. Generally, a grant will help this situation, but it will not solve the problem.

In light of these struggles, we have put in place development seminars, offered free of charge to nonprofits that sense a need to strengthen their approach to self-sustenance or that we have otherwise identified as good candidates for this subject. Organizations participating are asked to be represented by the chief executive officer, a board member, and the person most responsible for raising support. A full day or more is spent with about a dozen organizations at a time, led by a team of people experienced in development and sensitive to the special pressures of the audience. In many cases this experience has breathed new life into an organization's approach to fundraising, changing the priorities and culture for doing so. The costs for us, quite modest, have been highly leveraged beyond what a normal grant would be able to accomplish, all for the long-range good of the organization.

Another enrichment program, not tied to fundraising, is what we call Youth Workers Round Tables. The goals here are encouragement, networking, collaboration, and edification. About three times a year we invite people together who provide leadership to youth organizations. These are the folks in the trenches, doing great work on behalf of us all, but who often labor with little financial and moral support and with a sense of isolation as well. By bringing two or three dozen of such folks together for informal interactions, with a keynoter who understands and inspires the group, a large constituency in the region can be better off with healthier youth led by rejuvenated leaders. A grant could not accomplish this, but it is certainly a defensible activity in terms of using our assets for the good of our people.

Finally, we should not undervalue the role the regional foundation has in matchmaking, putting together organizations and people that may benefit greatly from exchanging ideas. This is one of the lowest-cost efforts, but it has the potential to yield very high benefits.

## *Trends and emphases of regional foundations*

It would not be reasonable to suggest that regional foundations, as a group, are all experiencing similar trends and emphases in their grantmaking and operations. Given the heterogeneous group they are, it would not even be possible to get a good reading of activities that would be representative of the group. Nevertheless, based on where we see ourselves coming from and moving toward, some brief comments can be made. Perhaps these comments are more prescriptive than prophetic.

Since knowing the region is fundamental to wise grantmaking, there is a need for regional foundations to increasingly value and depend on the vital role staff play in gaining information on the region and educating boards so that well-informed decisions can be made. More foundations are catching on to this and since the need is so obvious it is likely to become a future emphasis for many others.

Efforts beyond grantmaking are also playing a greater role at many foundations. Regional foundations are strategically positioned to be of service to their constituencies with matchmaker and convener functions and by offering workshops and seminars that help organizations toward greater self-sufficiency. Over recent years we have increased these efforts and others appear to be doing so as well. There is plenty of room for all to get in the act, for the special interests of different foundations can provide an overall enrichment to a region, helping to make it a much better and more productive place in which to live.

Certainly there is a trend toward providing larger grants. This is reasonable, given inflation rates, but it has also been spurred in recent years by a friendly stock market that has pushed the growth of foundation assets so that more is available to support worthy projects and programs at higher levels. It is a wonderful problem, both for grantseeker and grantmaker.

## *Summary*

Regional foundations, being less than national and more than single-state in the geographic areas they serve, have special challenges in getting to know their territories and special opportunities to support their constituencies. Although their primary task is giving grants, with a good knowledge of their regions these foundations can serve valuable convener and educational roles that can strengthen organizations in ways not easily done with grants.

NEAL O. THORPE *is executive director and trustee of the M. J. Murdock Charitable Trust, a general-purpose regional foundation headquartered in Vancouver, Washington.*

*In recent years, community foundations have quietly taken their place as the fastest-growing sector of American philanthropy. Eighty-five years after the first community foundation was established, every major metropolitan area of the United States now has at least one and some cities have several, and gifts, grants, and assets are growing at unprecedented rates.*

# 4

# Community foundations: Linking donors to communities

*Alicia A. Philipp*

COMMUNITY FOUNDATIONS range in size from small organizations with a few thousand dollars to the New York Community Trust with assets of over $1.5 billion. A 1997 survey of U.S. community foundations conducted by the Columbus Foundation reported that 547 community foundations now manage combined assets of $21.27 billion. Grants paid were at an all-time high of $1.255 billion, an increase of 25.5 percent above the landmark $1 billion in 1996. Last year, 33 foundations made grants of more than $10 million to improve the quality of life in their communities.

## *What is a community foundation?*

While it is difficult to arrive at a definition that covers all community foundations, they do have some features in common:

- *Geographic focus.* Most community foundations restrict their activities to particular metropolitan areas, although some, like the Oregon Community Foundation and the Rhode Island Foundation, operate statewide.
- *Public charity status.* This legal classification requires that a significant portion of the foundation's support come from a relatively large number of donors. Public charity status also gives donors maximum deductibility for their contributions. Many people establish funds within community foundations because it is a less expensive way to become involved with professionally managed philanthropy than to create a private foundation.
- *Representative nature of the board.* Whether public officials or private groups appoint board members, these boards seek to reflect the demographics of their community populations. The style of each community foundation is strongly influenced by this board leadership. In fact, because community foundations are public organizations and are therefore highly accountable, it could even be said that their boards play a stronger role in establishing policy and setting the directions for program activity than the boards of many other foundations.

In some ways, community foundations function as philanthropic brokers or clearinghouses. They raise funds from the private sector, manage them, and distribute them to eligible nonprofit organizations—and in some cases to individuals and local government agencies. Increasingly, during recent times some community foundations have also extended their roles to become catalysts for the discussion and resolution of community issues and problems.

## *How community foundations work*

Every community foundation has built its assets in a way that reflects its own history and leadership and those of its community. A number of community foundations (especially the oldest, like the ones in Cleveland and Hartford) have high percentages of *unrestricted* funds available for disbursements. Others, like the Baltimore foundation, have raised these kinds of monies with special capital campaigns. Donors to community foundations range from men and women who annually contribute a few thousand dollars to the very rich who may give or bequeath millions of dollars, either in unrestricted funds or for special purposes.

As a general rule, contributors make their gifts from accumulated assets rather than from their income. However, some community foundations work hard to encourage "populist philanthropy," contributions of small amounts from people with limited financial resources. This promotes a community-wide sense of ownership in the foundation.

Many community foundations that experienced significant growth during the 1980s (as in Atlanta), as well as some of the largest ones (in New York, for example), have a large portion of their assets in *donor-advised* funds. These funds permit living donors to participate actively in philanthropic decisions by recommending to community foundation boards the areas of need they want their resources to address. In these situations, the community foundation, knowing the donor's charitable interests, can suggest projects for funding. Sometimes the foundation, by drawing upon several donor-advised funds, can put together a package of support for a local nonprofit organization.

There are times when a community foundation may expand this concept more directly. Because of its knowledge of the local scene and particular needs, it may establish *field-of-interest* funds and publicize the opportunities for donors to pool their resources to address these needs. For example, community foundations have responded in this fashion to the needs of the homeless. Several of them have also created field-of-interest funds to support programs specifically targeted for women—a group that, historically, has received relatively low levels of support from the philanthropic community. Often these field-of-interest funds have specially appointed advisory committees that assist with both fundraising and grantmaking decisions.

Community foundations also manage *designated* funds, the income of which is earmarked for particular beneficiaries. This service is especially helpful for donors who want to designate specific recipients, but prefer not to turn over investment responsibilities to them. In this way, donors know that their funds will be managed well in perpetuity on behalf of their chosen charities.

There are several major trends that are currently shaping the continued development of community foundations in the United States.

## *Connecting donors and communities*

Helping others has always been part of the fabric of American society. Still, the needs in our communities continue to outpace our ability to address them. Regardless of the issue, the most fundamental challenge is how we connect people in need with those who have the resources and desire to help. And in an age of instantaneous global communication, the challenge is reaching people with the means to help when they are members of several communities, all competing for their attention.

Making these connections is an increasingly important part of the work of community foundations. The foundations help donors connect with organizations and leaders in areas of interest to them. They also seek to raise public awareness of key issues. Community foundations help connect nonprofit organizations with potential partners, mentors, and technical assistance to improve their effectiveness and long-term sustainability. They support the efforts of nonprofit leaders and institutions to connect with counterparts in government and the private sector.

Many of the needs community foundations seek to address require direct, highly focused local action, street by street in the case of rebuilding neighborhoods, or life by life in the case of children born to single parents who live in or near poverty. Other needs that transcend all boundaries can only be addressed on a regional basis, such as clean air, safe drinking water, rational transportation, and intelligent land use. Increasingly, community foundations are realizing the value of regional approaches to issues such as homelessness and affordable housing.

But whether a community need is neighborhood-specific or regional in scope, there are hundreds of touchpoints where the generosity of a single donor can make a difference. And yet these touchpoints would never be known to most donors without community foundations across the country. By working more personally with donors, community foundations can help them understand these touchpoint opportunities, identify areas where they can invest in solutions, and then make it happen on their behalf.

## *A new generation of philanthropists*

Few would argue with the assertion that there is a new generation of wealth in America today. Early results of research that the Community Foundation for Greater Atlanta is involved in reveal a wide diversity of ethnicity among the Atlanta region's wealthiest citizens, including where they live and how they have made their money.

These new philanthropists want a more "hands-on" approach to charitable giving and are interested in seeing their efforts have an impact. They embrace innovation and "out of the box" thinking and solutions, and they reward collaboration. They have fewer turf issues, involve their families in their charitable planning, and bring fresh perspectives from the innovative ways they have created their wealth.

For many community foundations, this means a more focused effort at "customer service" and a more delicate balance between meeting a donor's charitable objectives and leading that donor to new ways to meet those objectives. The Community Foundation for Greater Atlanta has been working for several years with a couple in their early forties interested in urban renewal and in developing a community in the heart of metro Atlanta. The result of their discussions with the Community Foundation created a local affiliate of a national nonprofit peer-lending group and provided funding to several nonprofit organizations working on issues of personal concern to them.

## *An expanded level of customer service*

Community foundations are not the only institutions ready to assist donors with their charitable giving objectives. An increasingly competitive environment for charitable dollars has created new partnerships with other financial institutions. Merrill Lynch & Company recently announced an alliance with community foundations nationwide that offers wealthy clients the choice of establishing individual funds that contribute to community foundations and benefit their communities directly.

Increased competition from for-profit financial organizations such as banks and other financial service organizations has created the need for community foundations to be clear about the value that their services add for current and potential donors. That is why many community foundations are moving to a more hands-on approach in the area of donor services, and why we need to continually look for new services to help these donors link to their communities. As more community foundations make donors their customers and services to donors their priority, they are realizing the importance of integrating all of the foundation's functions to serve donors' charitable objectives.

## *Catalysts for regional thinking*

Community foundations are one of the major players in helping their communities "think regionally" and "act locally." To that end, community foundations can be a bridge to moving regional agendas forward in metropolitan areas across the United States. Atlanta, for example, has become more than a city in traditional terms. It is now a region, spanning 20 counties, 103 cities, 227 local governing bodies, with dozens of distinctive geographic, ethnic, and cultural communities. By working closely with donors in the Atlanta area, the Community Foundation for Greater Atlanta aspired to enable a new generation of "regional citizens" who think of their communities in broad terms, and who take local actions that reach more deeply than ever before.

More than any organizations I know of, community foundations bring together people with vision, people willing to put aside their preconceptions and think boldly. These people bring the broadest range of perspectives to the table. Together with the foundations, they can help forge a framework that integrates economic, environmental, and social goals into the discussion and decision-making process in many communities.

This intensified role really plays to the community foundations' niche and greatest strength—an in-depth knowledge of their various communities. Community foundations have strong track records for discovering organizations that have the ideas, the energy, and the skills to effect important and innovative solutions.

Those of us who work in this unique sector of the philanthropic universe doubt whether there is any grant-making organization that is more accessible than a community foundation and its staff. Anyone who has labored in the fundraising vineyards knows the difficulties that can surround an approach to a government agency, a private or corporate foundation, or a wealthy individual.

By contrast, and as implied by its name, a community foundation is in business to serve the public—and that public is very broadly defined. For anyone with a great new project, an idea whose time has come, or simply a question about possible sources of support, the community foundation is an excellent way station on the fundraising pilgrimage. A review of the annual reports of most community foundations will attest to this accessibility.

Community foundation staff members readily make themselves available for appointments. They can offer suggestions about local philanthropy, volunteer information about projects similar to the one for which the visitor is seeking support, and make practical suggestions about fundraising steps and strategies.

## *Building partnerships for a new century*

The connections that community foundations are making today will continue to have an impact on future generations of Americans. As community foundations work with larger numbers of living donors, there will be increased opportunities for insights, experiences, and networks that can be as useful to the community as the funds they provide. In addition, those who have seen members of their community benefit from community foundation activities will be more likely to choose community foundations as a vehicle for their own charitable objectives when they seek productive uses for their newly accumulating wealth.

As charitable giving increases in social significance, more attention will be focused on what foundations are doing and how they are doing it. As an institution, community foundations have performed effectively over the years and are a vital force in American philanthropy. By binding donors and their families and community causes together to create powerful, effective matches, community foundations produce a positive impact on individuals, families, neighborhoods, and communities as a whole. Characterized by creativity, flexibility, inclusion, and independence, community foundations will continue to flourish in the new century as a necessary social process.

ALICIA A. PHILIPP *is executive director of the Community Foundation for Greater Atlanta, Inc.*

*A commitment to cooperative partnerships among private foundations, federal agencies, and universities can help bring about significant institutional change. Scenarios from academic organizations can also apply to other agencies.*

# 5

# Building alliances for institutional support

*Jeanne L. Narum*

EDUCATIONAL REFORM CANNOT OCCUR in a vacuum. As universities and colleges seek to develop, foster, and act on an institutional vision, they must build alliances with those outside their campus community. And in providing support for institutional reform, private foundations and government agencies will look to the vision behind the reform efforts—they want to know how the investment they will make fits into the institutional *Weltanschauung.*

As José Ortega y Gasset (1992) noted, we cannot live without ideas. Ideas determine our preferences, shape our values, guide our actions, and direct our lives. When we think about reforming our nation's colleges and universities, we are thinking about what we are willing to include in our universe of ideas, and about the choices we will make in "doing one thing instead of another." The process of institutional reform is driven by, and pulled by, institutional vision. Indeed, only a clear, decisive, and truthful understanding of a guiding vision will lead to clear, decisive, and truthful action.

NEW DIRECTIONS FOR PHILANTHROPIC FUNDRAISING, NO. 23, SPRING 1999 © JOSSEY-BASS PUBLISHERS

From the perspective of the campus community, then, the first step in constructing authentic alliances to further institutional goals is *clarity of purpose.* Faculty and their administrative colleagues must have a firm vision of the future in regard to strengthening the environment for learning for all students. There must be a clear sense of how efforts toward faculty, curricular, and institutional development play out in relation to that vision.

Ortega y Gasset spoke to the need for a mission, an idea, and a plan. I suggest that these are the critical benchmarks for alliances in developing as well as considering requests for external support in the work of functioning alliances. When the National Science Foundation asks applicants for a Career Award to present their "objectives and significance of the proposed integrated research and education activities," it is asking about vision—about mission and goals. When the American Honda Foundation asks a college president: "Is the program dreamful, imaginative, innovative, creative and humanistic?" it is asking about ideas. These funding sources, and all others, also ask for a plan, for why you are doing one thing rather than another, given the mission and ideas driving the project.

## *Building alliances*

A shared vision is the point at which to begin. A shared vision about educational purpose helps align partners' questions about goals and outcomes. A shared vision helps address key questions that need to be asked by all potential partners in the alliance:

- How will this particular investment of resources make a difference?
- To whom will it make a difference?
- How will we know?

### *Institutional missions*

A clearly articulated vision from the academic institution can help partners rally around commonly agreed-upon goals. Even generic catalogue statements can drive the process:

At its simplest, a liberal education teaches the basic skills upon which higher achievements rest: to read perceptively, to write and speak clearly, and to think analytically. Carleton College draws upon these skills to foster a critical appreciation of our intellectual, aesthetic, and moral heritage and to encourage original thought.

[Skidmore College has] consistently espoused the goal of liberal education as the best means of preparing for a life of continuing personal growth and of responsible and significant service of the community.

In an open society, upward mobility is an obvious and attainable goal for each member of the population. Upward mobility is usually based upon improved education. . . . Universidad Metropolitana's [Puerto Rico] mission is to provide its students, within an atmosphere of academic freedom, the necessary resources to help develop mental flexibility, intellectual curiosity and linguistic ability as tools for their professional and for their daily lives.

These excerpts from institutional catalogues speak about the role of education in a democracy, and therefore provide a basis for a claim on private and public support to further that mission. They help explain why faculty and their administrative colleagues think it possible to ask private and corporate foundations, as well as government agencies, to invest in their ideas. Indeed, what academics quickly find out in initial conversations with prospective supporters (private and public alike) is that they see funding specific projects from such a broader, visionary perspective.

### *Missions of foundations*

It is important in this regard to focus also on what the potential alliance partners are saying about their mission. To wit:

The guiding purpose of the [Camille and Henry Dreyfus] Foundation . . . is to advance the science of chemistry, chemical engineering and related sciences as a means of improving human relations and circumstances around the world.

When W. M. Keck established the W. M. Keck Foundation in 1954, he foresaw a philanthropic institution that would apply creativity and imagination to provide far-reaching benefits for humanity in the narrow but seemingly fathomless disciplines of science and engineering, medical research, and higher education.

### *Missions of federal agencies*

Similar sentiments can be found in announcements from federal agencies:

> [The National Science Foundation's long-range goals are to] enable the U.S. to uphold a position of world leadership in all aspects of science, mathematics, and engineering . . . promote the discovery, integration, dissemination, and employment of new knowledge in service to society; achieve excellence in U.S. [SME&T] education at all levels [National Science Foundation, 1996].

> Democracy demands wisdom and vision in its citizens. . . . while no government can call a great artist into existence, it is necessary and appropriate for the Federal Government to help create and sustain not only a climate encouraging freedom of thought, imagination, and inquiry, but also the material conditions facilitating the release of this creative talent [National Foundation on the Arts and the Humanities Act of 1965, p. 845].

Each of these missions is noble, focusing on the renewal of society. Yet, eloquent as they are, they only set the stage for building alliances working *to make a difference.* It takes strategic planning; it takes connections and channels of communication that link academics with good ideas to those with dollars to invest in good ideas. Policies and procedures that serve needs and goals of all partners and hard work on all sides are needed to trigger critical support in a timely fashion.

Since there is not and never will be enough money to support all worthy projects (those excellent ideas that hit the desk of those with dollars to distribute), as a first step we should remember that alliances with potential partners bring faculty and institutions benefits beyond the purely financial.

## *Understanding the benefits of alliances*

Authentic alliances offer many benefits, including opportunities for exchanging and clarifying ideas, for advice to the prospective grantee, and for the creation of connections that apply beyond a single project. Even individual faculty seeking support for their scholarly activities find they must respond to a whole raft of questions, including ones about connections and timeliness:

- How does the proposed project relate to your work with students, with broader curriculum developments on your campus, with new directions in your disciplinary community?
- Is this a new venture or the next logical step in an extended project? Why does this have to be done now—at your present career stage, in relation to work done by others in your field, for its potential to contribute to current curriculum reforms on your campus?

### *Advice and counsel*

Similar questions could be asked of institution-wide projects. One value of an alliance comes at an early stage, perhaps even at the point of pressing to get an initial hearing for an idea. Advice from staffers in the process of developing a proposal may help keep potential applicants from reinventing wheels or from making unsupportable claims about the uniqueness of a particular approach or hypothesis. Critical review of an idea at an initial stage, either by peers or by experienced professional staffers, can sharpen and reshape that idea toward the end of a better project—be it preparing a multivolume translation of the writings of the Danish philosopher Søren Kierkegaard or renovating spaces for scientific research.

An outsider can also ask the hard questions: Why does this have to be done now? Why are you the right person to do it? Or perhaps even the more direct, *So what?*—once posed in National Endowment for the Humanities program guidelines as the key question to be addressed by potential applicants and reviewers.

### *External review*

Another benefit comes at the end of the process, after the decision has been made and comments communicated. An NSF staffer once suggested to me that the process should be seen as an opportunity for an external review, to gain advice from experts in the field. This might be small solace for a rejected applicant (either individual or institutional), but those who succeed over the long term are those who continue to reexamine their answers to the *Why me?* and *Why now?* questions, to articulate how and to whom the project will make a difference, and to press their case.

A functioning alliance also assumes that the academic partner will pay attention to comments in the letter of declination. For example, reviewer comments like these suggest more than a rewriting will be necessary if the idea is to find eventual support:

- "The proposal conveys almost no evidence of institutional capacity."
- "The proposal is too broadly defined; it outlines activities that are simply too ambitious to be completed during the proposed project period."
- "I am concerned that the project lacks perspective. Why is this important, how will this research advance our understanding of the field?"

Indeed, a National Endowment for the Humanities program officer once grumbled to me, "Some faculty seem to think it is all a lottery; you just keep trying until your lucky number comes up."

### *Connections*

A useful alliance is also one where connections are made: to people doing similar work, to those with appropriate expertise to help plan, implement, and assess a project, and to connections for future funding. Many funding agencies, including the Howard Hughes Medical Institute, the Fund for the Improvement of Postsecondary Education (U.S. Department of Education), and the M. J. Murdock Charitable Trust, regularly host meetings of grantees. These are opportunities to share materials as well as ideas for adapting in other settings; they also put the spotlight on persons doing interesting work in regard to program evaluation, dissemination, outreach, and other efforts.

### *Investments*

But ideas, comments, and connections are not the major reason to pursue alliances (at least those that lead to the renewal of society, the advancement of knowledge, the transformation of institutions). Valuable alliances are created when good ideas and dollars to invest in good ideas come together, wherein all partners understand the responsibilities and obligations of the others.

## *Designing a strategic itinerary*

Having a goal assumes a plan to achieve that goal. I propose we think about designing a strategic itinerary as a means to think about building alliances, understanding the need for carefully wrought timetables and benchmarks against which to measure progress. The concept of itineraries illustrates a recognition of the various options at hand to reach a goal. Academics, who most often initiate this process, know there are a great many public and private funding sources, each with its own goals and practices. Presidents and faculty also know that when confronted with a request for money, funding sources will ask:

- Is this request consistent with our goals?
- Given the great number of demands on our resources, would supporting this request be the best investment we can make at this time?

### *Identifying potential partners*

The initial step in the journey for faculty and their administrative colleagues is to identify those potential funding partners who answer yes to the question, *Is this request consistent with our goals?* It is in this group that partners will be found to help shape their future. And here is where the process *can* become complicated.

Obviously, preparing a competitive proposal is essential. No support will be forthcoming without a document of substance, one that articulates a timely, institutionally appropriate need, together with a carefully thought-out plan of attack—all in clear, elegant, and persuasive language.

### *Dealing with complexity*

The process is complex because the needs and goals of the academic community are multidimensional. Colleges and universities seek gifts and grants to support new curricular initiatives in international studies, a campuswide teaching and learning center, or the purchase of major scientific instrumentation. Individual faculty wishing to stay at the cutting edge in disciplinary or pedagogical research look for support for their scholarly efforts. Academic institutions pursue private gifts to match federal dollars; they look for pilot support from a local foundation to set the stage for a larger request from a national organization.

Collectively, the objectives and practices of the funding community are also multidimensional. Private foundations and governmental agencies have different parameters in regard to size, duration, timing, as well as purpose of a grant: seed money, operating support, capstone, or challenge grants. Some give both to individuals and institutions; others have restrictions as to who can receive support. Many have funding priorities established by law or by their articles of incorporation. There are those with regular deadlines or RFPs, and others that are flexible in responding to requests, in regard to deadlines as well as to types of projects supported. It is this very diversity of potential partners that makes the process of building alliances an adventurous journey. As Alan Pifer notes, "Every agency which can serve the common good by facilitating the processes of institutional change toward a more just, healthier, better educated, and more universally prosperous national and world society has a very special value" (1973).

### *Dealing with people*

It is important to note that people with dollars give to people with ideas, that there is a very personal dimension to the building of alliances. A federal staffer with responsibility for major fellowships once told me, "We don't fund projects, we fund careers." Even at this large, seemingly impersonal agency, there is visible concern about the future of individuals and institutions presenting their case; again and again, federal program officers invite prospective applicants to visit, to present initial ideas, to engage their expertise in the evolution of the project. Many academics are surprised (pleasantly) that ideas outside the mainstream can be entertained—that these staffers are looking for the best and that they recognize the conceivable limitations of current RFPs. This flexibility is also evident in the giving approach at some private and corporate foundations. Indeed, such funders as the Exxon Education Foundation work closely with prospective grantees, aiming to invest in projects that have substantial impact over the long term.

## *Sample itineraries*

The scenarios that follow illustrate itineraries; they highlight the multidimensional nature of institutional needs and goals, and the importance of having a mission, an idea, and a plan.

### *Scenario I*

It is August. A newly appointed member of the chemistry faculty is having lunch with his dean. There is a culture on this campus that recognizes that the interactive combination of teaching and scholarship—most satisfying to a teacher-scholar—is also the most engaging education for students. This culture shapes how faculty are brought into the community and how their careers are nurtured.

The topic for the lunch meeting is *writing proposals*, in the context of a broader discussion about scholarship. The division expects all faculty to prepare proposals seeking support for their professional work; indeed, this young chemist has both received $50,000 in start-up funds and had one course released to develop an agenda for seeking and securing support for his work.

From her own experience, the dean knows writing proposals is essential to having a vital career. She has used the proposal-writing process to shape and reshape her long-term plans, keep visibly active within her disciplinary community, and enrich her work with students in classroom and lab. Over the past several years, her faculty have had remarkable success in securing external support for their scholarly efforts. Gifts and grants have ranged from $5,000 from a regional pharmaceutical company to four awards from the NSF Faculty Early Career Development Program. Some grants were seed money for new directions in research; another made possible an extended leave for collaborative research overseas. Current gifts and grants to the division are from over twenty different foundations, agencies, and corporations.

The dean describes the experience of divisional colleagues, stressing the need for a systematic approach to building a career. She asks the young chemist to determine what he would like to accomplish in the next five years and identify everything it will take to achieve those goals—from a single piece of instrumentation to three solid months in an industrial lab. At the next lunch, the dean and the new chemist will go over his plans, and begin to link specific funding opportunities with particular needs. They will begin to lay the building blocks for his career.

### *Scenario II*

It is the regular meeting of the college's senior staff. The agenda is to review current progress toward the goal of having international and cross-cultural experiences at the center of the learning for all students, and to outline the next phase of development. The associate vice president for development is new, so they describe the history of the decision to make international and cross-cultural studies an institutional hallmark. The catalyst for the decision was a serendipitous discussion twelve years ago among a small group of faculty with a common interest in language, literature, and cultural studies. The discussion led to broader departmental discussions, to a small grant from the dean for a team-taught course, and ultimately to the establishment of a collegewide planning task force to set new curricular endeavors in place.

Over the past ten years, involved faculty and development officers have worked to:

- Craft a short statement of long-range goals.
- Outline needs in the areas of faculty development, programmatic development, and instructional technologies to meet those goals.
- Identify potential sources of support.
- Develop and implement a plan to pursue those sources in a timely manner.

The initial potential supporters for faculty development included federal programs such as the Fulbright Scholars Program; over the past six years, seven faculty had Fulbrights. The internal endowment for faculty development provides supplemental assistance as needed; merit increases are pegged to the contribution that faculty are making to achieve the broader institutional goals set by the vote of the faculty. A seven-figure request for faculty development activities linked to this initiative is now on the desk of a major national foundation.

Programmatic development was advanced with three grants from the National Endowment for the Humanities: first one for summer planning, then a three-year grant to develop a series of team-taught courses linked to study-abroad programs, and finally a major challenge grant to provide an endowment to support faculty development and related library acquisitions over the long term. The institutional credibility gained through the National Endowment for the Humanities Challenge triggered gifts and grants from a wide range of donors who recognized that such a grant was one benchmark of success. The challenge for the next stage is to more directly address technology needs.

## *Using itineraries*

The faculty and administrators in the scenarios presented here were busy figuring out how to facilitate institutional change. In the first instance, the dean was working to ensure that faculty maintained an active research agenda that infected students and infused the curriculum with the joy of discovery. The focus in the second was on challenging all students to understand the ways and thinking of people in different times and places—and connect those understandings to their life beyond the campus. These are both costly endeavors over the long term. The script for these scenarios only begins to suggest the complexity of building alliances, how it takes both careful and creative planning, some risk-taking (perhaps on all sides), openness, and trust.

### *Focusing on the goal*

Developing strategic itineraries is one approach to uncomplicating the process. Itineraries will reflect that when academics look for partners to support an idea, they know they must:

- Have a clear goal in mind, one that is obvious to members of the campus community as well as to potential funding sources.
- Know there is more than one route to the goal.
- Realize it may take many smaller efforts to achieve the goal. These may be parallel efforts or sequential, depending on the resources available.
- Have a careful plan that covers all possible scenarios.

What an itinerary can do is help academic leaders in visualizing the workaday reality of building alliances—in establishing timetables and benchmarks to get from here to there. Some further scenarios will be illustrative here.

### *Planning multiple routes*

Deans and department chairs who have a goal of assembling a faculty of effective and creative scholars (committed equally to student learning and to their own research, demonstrably capable in both arenas) can link and leverage support from a variety of sources to achieve that goal. They will know they need to define many different routes toward that end, to serve needs of faculty at various career stages, within different disciplines, as well as at a particular point in balancing teaching, research, and service obligations. Different approaches will make it possible to serve the collective needs of the campus as well as the needs of individual faculty members, while staying focused on the goal. Institutions with such a vision should note aims of an important National Science Foundation program:

> To sustain and strengthen the Nation's science, mathematics, and engineering capabilities and to promote the use of those capabilities in service to society, the [National Science Foundation (NSF)] is dedicated to strengthening linkages among individuals and institutions committed to progress in research and education and to fostering the natural connections between the processes of learning and discovery. NSF aims to encourage integrated environments for research and education in which education is infused with the joy of discovery and research is informed by the needs of the learning process [National Science Foundation, 1997, p. 3].

Experience from current alliances will serve to illustrate the value of itineraries.

### *Scenario III*

With support from a private foundation, this college has established an endowed fund that makes an annual grant to a pre-tenure faculty member for three years of support for scholarly activities that link research, teaching, and service in ways parallel to those underwritten by the NSF Career Program. There is intense competition each year for these prestigious internal grants, but even the unsuccessful applicants value the process—and many of them have later successfully submitted their proposals to either the National Science Foundation or the National Endowment for the Humanities.

### *Scenario IV*

A college in the south has just completed a successful major capital campaign. Over the course of the effort, significant gifts have been made by those private foundations within their alliance. Now, in planning for their future, faculty, deans, and development officers look to federal opportunities to support new programs. Their first look is at the Fund for the Improvement of Postsecondary Education, one of the few potential partners that publicly takes risks, as many new ideas are starting to emerge from programs established and expanded during the capital campaign. They are also considering the National Endowment for the Humanities Focus Grant Program, which supports small groups of faculty studying texts and exploring new pedagogical approaches, working together to outline a new departmental course or interdisciplinary program. There is a strong sense throughout the community that good ideas can lead to good projects, and campus leaders want to sustain that interest and enthusiasm in the search for external support.

### *Scenario V*

Other scenarios could be developed from stories of institutions that were challenged by an invitation from the Howard Hughes Medical Institute to incorporate outreach into their planned activities as they sought HHMI support, toward the end serving "two primary goals: production of the finest scientists for the 21st century and raising the scientific and technological literacy of all Americans" (Howard Hughes Medical Institute, 1997).

### *Scenario VI*

Lessons can be learned from colleges and universities that have woven the search for external support (alliances) into institutional policies and practices. Some require that a sabbatical application include mention of applying for fellowships to the American Council of Learned Societies, the National Endowment for the Humanities, the National Science Foundation, the Council for the International Exchange of Scholars, and perhaps even the Deutscher Akademischer Austauschdiesnst (German Academic Exchange Service). Another approach is to ask that annual internal equipment budget requests be accompanied by the same argument and rationale that would be included in a proposal to a government agency.

These are all steps toward enhancing faculty skills in proposal preparation, and thus a more competitive stream of proposals from that institution. Establishing institutional matching funds for faculty grants also encourages faculty with ideas to take risks, knowing there will be a reward for their extra efforts and creativity.

We could also develop scenarios from the perspective of other partners, for example about the value of the peer review from a federal agency in the process of making funding decisions. In many ways, the templates for proposal preparation and review for governmental agencies are of benefit across the alliance.

## *Thinking about the future*

How might these scenarios be different five to ten years from now? How will the current emphasis on accountability and stewardship—*how will you know you've made a difference?*—affect the building and sustaining of alliances? Will those colleges and universities that are aggressively documenting the difference new programs are making on student learning, faculty productivity, and institutional cultures have it easier than those that are not? In a time of shrinking resources and increasing needs, will there be funding partners willing to take risks with an idea that is more exploratory than certain? Will institutions become conservative in the ideas they present for consideration, assuming that such will be more competitive? Do private and public funders see themselves as agents of change, or responsible only for strengthening institutions with demonstrated success? Will we arrive at some creative balance between the need for innovation and the need for continuity? How, in a time of uncertain public trust of higher education, can colleges and universities continue to make the case that a strong undergraduate community serves the interests of society? Will there be an increasing number of alliances that include multiple academic partners, as well as multiple funding partners—toward the end of serving societal goals more creatively and efficiently?

> To tell the people we must renew America and then to ignore the need for a clear policy and adequate funding in education is to invite eventually the people's collective derision. The tough realities of America's future, and the historical principles on which that future must be based, demand a clear voice and responsible assistance. Schools and the means of education are among our most precious assets—too important to be left to the federal government, too important not to be fostered by our national leadership in appropriate and imaginative ways [Giamatti, 1988].

## *Conclusion*

The history of American higher education would be quite different without the tradition of private philanthropy that has served this country well from the time of the colonial colleges to our own day. In this century, public support of colleges and universities—through government agencies, foundations, and endowments—has become a key factor in enabling institutions of higher education to build and sustain quality programs that serve society most creatively and effectively.

Now—and well into the next century—the colleges and universities that prosper will be those that manage to link and leverage private and public support. Institutions that prosper will create alliances in support of their mission and of their future in the form of gifts and grants, while honoring the proper roles of individual partners within the alliance. The common commitment of private foundations, public funding agencies, and academic institutions to work toward a more just and prosperous society opens the door for such alliances.

### *References*

Giamatti, A. B. *A Free and Ordered Space: The Real World of the University.* New York: Norton, 1988.

Howard Hughes Medical Institute. *Grants for Science Education.* 1997.
National Foundation on the Arts and the Humanities Act of 1965 (P. L. 89–208, Sept. 28, 1965).
National Science Foundation. *NSF Faculty Early Career Development Program Guidelines.* Washington, D. C.: National Science Foundation, 1997.
National Science Foundation. *Strategic Plan.* Washington, D. C.: National Science Foundation, 1996.
Ortega y Gasset, J. *Mission of the University.* (Rev. ed.) New Brunswick, N.J.: Transaction, 1992. (Originally published 1944.)
Pifer, A. *The Future of Foundations.* 1973.

JEANNE L. NARUM *is the founding director of Project Kaleidoscope. She is responsible for developing and coordinating various facets of the project, including the Faculty for the Twenty-First Century as well as seminars and publications on facilities planning and workshops and events on disciplinary, topical, and institutional issues.*

*The traditional definition of international grantmakers' support for peace and security projects has broadened to include health, education, and human rights programs. Foundations can also help educate Americans about the role of investing resources in cooperative international efforts to solve global problems.*

# 6

# Challenges of international grantmaking

*Colin G. Campbell, Priscilla Lewis*

TO SUGGEST THAT PATTERNS in foundation grantmaking are influenced by large social, intellectual, economic, and political developments is to state the obvious. After all, such developments help define the challenges and problems foundations set out to address, and the strategic opportunities that are available to them. In the domestic sphere, for example, the politics of devolution—the transfer of responsibility for ensuring vital social services from the federal to state and local governments, and from the public sector to the private—have placed new demands on community groups and on private philanthropy, causing many U.S. foundations to reconsider their grantmaking strategies and the distribution of their resources.

But when those large developments are sufficiently sweeping, unprecedented, and complex, the nature of their influence on

NEW DIRECTIONS FOR PHILANTHROPIC FUNDRAISING, NO. 23, SPRING 1999 © JOSSEY-BASS PUBLISHERS

foundation grantmaking becomes far from obvious. Such has been the case in the international sphere over the past decade, a time of enormous social and geopolitical change. The end of the Cold War, the opening of Central and Eastern Europe, the transition to democracy in South Africa, the acceleration of global economic integration, the worldwide expansion of the NGO sector—these and other profoundly important developments have had a complicated impact on international grantmaking in the United States. These massive shifts have called not only for changes in grantmaking emphasis and strategy, but also, in many respects, for a reconsideration of the very terms and categories of international grantmaking itself.

After reviewing the highlights of a recent comprehensive study of international grantmaking, this chapter explores in greater depth one of the major categories of international grantmaking—international affairs, peace, and security—to provide a more vivid picture of the ferment that characterizes international grantmaking today. It then draws some general conclusions about trends in international grantmaking, and considers the special role of foundations in addressing the challenges of a globalized and increasingly interdependent world.

## *Overview of international grantmaking*

What does the field of international grantmaking look like today? In fact, this is not an easy question to answer. To the extent that foundations are responding to new global needs and opportunities, in newly accessible regions, their activities are more difficult to track and categorize (as will be discussed in more detail in the section that follows). There has also been a lag in compiling information, which is frustrating—if inevitable—at a time of such rapid change. The very useful 1997 Foundation Center study from which most of the statistics in this chapter are drawn, for example, ends with 1994 data; since then, several major foundations have restructured their international grantmaking programs (Renz and others, 1997).

According to the Foundation Center study, overall foundation funding grew a healthy 14 percent, adjusted for inflation, between 1990 and 1994—from $8.7 billion to $11.3 billion. International funding, which includes both giving in the United States for international activities and giving throughout the world, rose almost $200 million to an estimated $966 million in 1994—somewhat under 9 percent of the total, with an inflation-adjusted gain of 11.3 percent since 1990. Within the Foundation Center's study sample of more than a thousand larger foundations whose grantmaking represented over 50 percent of all foundation giving in 1994 and more than two-thirds of all estimated international giving that year, gains in international funding were much higher—18 percent in real terms—and exactly matched the growth rate for all funding. International funding by the sample foundations amounted to 11.5 percent of all giving by those foundations, the same share as in 1990.

At somewhere around 10 percent or 11 percent of overall foundation giving, then, international grantmaking has doubled since the early 1980s, when it was estimated at about 5 percent of all giving, but has leveled off in the early and mid-1990s. At 10 percent or 11 percent of total giving, it must also be said, international programs do not represent a major priority of the more than forty thousand grantmaking foundations—large and small, independent, corporate, family, and community—in the United States. While nearly half of the Foundation Center's study sample of about 1,000 larger foundations made at least one international grant in 1994, only 153 foundations devoted at least a tenth of their grantmaking to international programs; 75 devoted at least a quarter of their grantmaking to international programs, and just 31 devoted half or more.

Based on further analysis of the study sample, the Foundation Center reports that international grantmakers have responded to post–Cold War changes by becoming far more active overseas. Funding of overseas recipients grew five times faster than funding of U.S.-based international programs from 1990 to 1994, reflecting no doubt the explosive growth of the NGO sector in many countries where such citizen-driven, independent activity had been suppressed or unimaginable for decades. Grantmaking to indigenous organizations in Central and Eastern Europe and in the former Soviet Union, for example, increased significantly from 1990 to 1994, as it did in sub-Saharan Africa and Latin America. U.S.-based programs received 57 percent of all grants in 1994, down from 67 percent in 1990. In 1995, the Foundation Center reported that the share of grants going to U.S.-based programs dropped even lower, to 37 percent, but in 1996 it returned to slightly over half of the total.

The increased involvement of funders with indigenous, grassroots groups has produced a more diversified array of international grantmaking programs, as foundations take on local issues and try to respond to local needs. Funding has increased at the grassroots level, reports the Foundation Center, for community improvement and human service programs, primary health care programs, primary and secondary education, adult and continuing education programs, media and communications, historic preservation, the performing arts, migration and refugee issues, and civil liberties. In a related development, funding is also on the rise for "special population groups"—women and girls, immigrants and refugees, children, minorities, people with AIDS, substance abusers, the economically disadvantaged, victims of crime and abuse. Like domestic grantmaking programs, interestingly enough, international grantmaking programs seem to be becoming more focused and more localized.

Also notable in the 1990s have been changes in the broad funding priorities of foundations with international programs. During the Cold War and through the 1980s, international affairs, peace, and security had been the primary funding area for international grantmakers. In the 1990s, according to the Foundation Center, "sweeping geopolitical changes caused funders to reassess their international programs, and dramatic shifts occurred." Grantmaking for international affairs declined, particularly for policy and research, exchanges, and peace and security. Within the peace and security subfield, funding for national security programs waned while support increased for arms control and for conflict resolution, one of the fastest-growing areas of international grantmaking. As funding of programs in the international affairs category dropped off, marked increases were recorded in the categories of international development (by 1994 this was the leading field of grantmaking), health and family planning, education, and human rights and civil liberties.

These reassessments and shifts in priorities are worthy of more extended consideration. The next section of this chapter will be devoted to taking a closer look at the status of international affairs, peace, and security grantmaking. Trends in this particular field—formerly the largest and still the third-largest category of international grantmaking—are illustrative of many of the changes and challenges that confront international funders, and indeed all organizations or agencies that are concerned with global problem solving in today's interdependent world.

## *Trends in security-related grantmaking*

The Rockefeller Brothers Fund (RBF) is one of those foundations that have decided to rethink their international programs, and specifically their security and security-related grantmaking. In the RBF's case, this rethinking involved temporarily suspending the Fund's security grantmaking in 1996 and undertaking a two-year effort to encourage and learn from a broad dialogue among scholars and policy shapers about the new threats to and requirements of security in the post–Cold War world—a world in which bipolar conflict is no longer the dominant theme and in which long-range, underlying trends of globalization, technological innovation, and environmental strain are coming to the fore (Pasic, 1998).

In this world, the Fund has learned, security can no longer be equated solely with the military security of the state. The question of whose security matters—nations? individuals? communities?

cultures or civilizations?—is newly open to debate, and a new set of threats and challenges has risen to prominence in the post–Cold War era:

- Globalization, which presents very real opportunities for improving the well-being of people around the world, also poses a host of new problems that respect no national borders, from rapid environmental degradation to international crime to the spread of infectious diseases.
- The Asian financial crisis has provoked a spate of articles pointing to the untrammeled international flow of capital—made possible by the revolution in information technology—as a danger against which even the most well-armed nation cannot defend itself.
- Other problems, like ethnic division and the division between the haves and the have-nots, are perhaps not really new but rather newly visible and newly pressing, now that they are out from under the pervasive Cold War cloud of superpower conflict.

The severity of these problems and the apparent inadequacy of our existing strategies and resources to deal with them suggest that, like widespread military combat, they pose real threats to the ability of nations and societies to sustain themselves—they are threats to security, in other words. Security, viewed in this broader fashion, is about the peaceful management of rapid and constant change—political, environmental, social, economic, technological. Ensuring this kind of security will require new institutional arrangements, new intellectual constructs, and new attitudes and approaches within the public and private sectors alike. The new Global Security grantmaking guidelines that were ultimately adopted by the fund in early 1999 rest on just such a broadened conception of security, a conception that links security to longstanding RBF interests in encouraging sustainable resource use and strengthening civil society. The full text of these guidelines is available on the Fund's Web site at [www.rbf.org].

The experiences of the RBF and of several other foundations that have been rethinking their security programs suggest that the documented decline in foundation support for international affairs, peace, and security actually masks—and points to—a more complex trend in security-related grantmaking. According to this reading, it is not so much funders' level of interest in security that is changing, but rather their definition of security. Although no consensus has been reached on a new formal definition of security—and many now assert that the pursuit of such a definition is both futile and beside the point—broad notions of "human security" and "environmental security," which encompass the economic, social, and political aspects as well as the military aspects of people's well-being and safety from harm, have achieved wide informal acceptance among funders, opinion leaders, and policymakers.

So it is not surprising that while grantmaking in the area of traditional security has declined, it is on the upswing in precisely those areas—international development, health and education, and human rights—where one might expect to find solutions to some of the new security problems. Increased attention to these program areas, therefore, ought not to be interpreted primarily as a loss of foundation interest in security and its replacement by other interests, but rather as an expression of misgiving about the capacity of traditional concepts to capture the changing nature of security, and as an exploration of newly perceived relationships among security and other international issues. In short, foundations' security agendas have broadened beyond traditional international affairs, peace, and security grantmaking and now overlap with other international grantmaking areas.

Along with a broadened conception of security has come a broadened array of players and partners on the international security stage. Just as it is no longer only nations whose security matters, so it is no longer—and in fact, has not been for some time—only nations that have the responsibility and the capacity to play a major role in ensuring security. National governments are still significant players, of course, as are international and multinational organizations like the United Nations and ASEAN. But one of the most remarkable security-related developments of recent years has been the emergence of powerful nonstate actors—including NGOs, other civil society organizations, and corporations—that are capable of advancing or undermining world security, sustainability, and quality of life. The recent negotiations over an international ban on land mines are a striking example of this phenomenon.

Foundations interested in security issues, broadly defined, are thus beginning to act in partnership with—and when appropriate, to make grants to—a much wider variety of organizations in the United States and abroad, including grassroots and national citizens' groups, international NGOs, business associations, and government agencies. Traditional distinctions among these organizations' roles and levels of involvement in international affairs are quickly breaking down. Where community security or human security are at issue (with respect to food safety or contagious disease threats, for example), it may be vital to work simultaneously with local civil society groups, national policy research institutes, and governmental or quasi-governmental entities.

As norms of democracy and self-determination take hold, the general public, too, is becoming a partner in addressing security issues. Here at home, since the United States is still uniquely capable of accelerating or obstructing international progress on security-related issues, building American constituencies for cooperative solutions to international problems—from the burgeoning small arms trade to global warming to the growing gap between rich and poor nations—will ultimately be as critical to ensuring world peace and well-being as supporting the efforts of indigenous NGOs in affected countries. The Rockefeller Brothers Fund is joining with several other international grantmakers to launch such a constituency-building effort, called the Global Interdependence Initiative, which will seek to stimulate a broad dialogue around Americans' basic values and preferences regarding their country's role in the world.

In fact, as the world becomes more interdependent, the very distinction between domestic and international aspects of security is blurring. It is suggestive, for example, that funding for national security programs per se has declined, according to the Foundation Center report, while support has increased for programs that focus on conflict resolution—an approach to violence prevention that has as strong a potential for domestic application as it does for international applications. What happens here in the United States, for good or for ill, has important consequences globally, and what happens in other countries will have significant direct or indirect effects on the United States. America's profligate use of energy contributes to environmental degradation worldwide, for example; poverty and financial crisis in developing nations severely limit the expansion of markets for American products. In an interconnected world, U.S. domestic policies (regarding workplace health and safety, for example) may ultimately have important implications for U.S. foreign policy (in this instance, trade policy).

U.S. foreign policy, as in the case of economic sanctions, will almost certainly affect conditions here at home. For this reason, helping American citizens learn to understand and address the impact of globalization on their communities, and to recognize the impact of their own actions and choices on communities halfway around the world, may well come to be viewed as an important security-related goal of international grantmaking—although the difficulties that might be encountered in categorizing such a program are themselves illustrative of the flux and ferment that surround this issue.

## *Challenges for international grantmaking*

What do these observations about security grantmaking suggest about international grantmaking in general? Most of the trends discussed thus far are in fact evident across the board in international grantmaking.

The broadening and integration of program areas, for example, and the growing importance of relationships among issues and issue categories are themes that have emerged throughout international grantmaking. As has also become evident in domestic grantmaking (in troubled urban areas, for example), problems rarely exist in isolation and effective solutions are almost always multifaceted and multidimensional. Like security, then, several of the other major international grantmaking agendas have broadened and begun to overlap significantly with other traditional program areas. International development is no longer just about building dams and bridges and encouraging agricultural innovation, or even just about improving the economies of developing countries; the notion of development has now been enlarged to include a set of related goals, including sustainability, equity, and cultural sensitivity.

Grantmaking designed to strengthen civil society, or to ensure a community voice in resource management and development planning, or to strengthen the rule of law and monitor the behavior of multinational corporations and multilateral lending agencies: all these may now be considered development-related activities. Social, environmental, and cultural considerations are increasingly being brought onto the development agenda because it has become evident that these considerations are in fact interrelated and that only a more comprehensive approach will produce the desired long-range results. The human rights agenda, for its part, has been enlarged to include a more deliberate emphasis on economic and social rights as well as civil and political rights. Human rights grantmaking, more broadly conceived, thus cuts across and overlaps education concerns, development concerns, and health and human security concerns.

Not surprisingly, several of the emerging program areas for international grantmaking that were identified by the Foundation Center are equally cross-cutting. Strengthening governance and civil society, promoting philanthropy, and educating the American public about international issues are all themes that cut across issue areas and beneficiary groups. Even the increasing focus on special beneficiary groups, such as women or children, may be regarded as a way of linking separate but related areas of concern—health, education, human rights, economic development—as they affect a certain population.

All this is not to suggest that international grantmaking categories, as traditionally defined, have never overlapped until now, or that those program categories are meaningless—or, for that matter, that "program areas" as such can ever be more than imprecise measures of the distribution of grant dollars. It does suggest, however, that a more holistic and comprehensive approach to issues and challenges may be gaining ground in international grantmaking—at the price of some clarity in definitions, categories, and conceptual frameworks.

Security is also not the only international program area in which new partners and new players have emerged. A broader conception of the development challenge, for example, requires a broader array of resources, talents, and experience with which to address it. As different types of challenges are increasingly perceived to be linked, so it will be increasingly necessary to adopt problem-solving approaches that link different kinds of skill and insight, from whatever sector or community. While continuing to monitor the policies and practices of the World Bank, for example, the RBF and a number of other international grantmakers have been exploring areas of concern they share with the Bank. The RBF and the Rockefeller, Joyce Mertz-Gilmore, MacArthur, and Heinz foundations have joined with the Bank—and will eventually be joined by private investors—to launch a stand-alone Solar Development Corporation, which will provide financing and business advisory services to accelerate the development of a market infrastructure for the distribution of household solar systems in rural areas of the developing world. Such collaborations are not confined to the development arena. The popularity of "cross-sectoral partnership" as a topic of conversation whenever international donors and NGOs assemble reflects an awareness that no single actor or type of action can resolve complex international or global problems—especially since the capacity and indeed the will of national governments to take the lead in ensuring such resolution is everywhere in doubt.

Finally, the blurring of distinctions between domestic and international, local and global issues is not confined to the security category of international grantmaking. Globalization—the rapid and increasingly unconstrained flow of people, capital, and information across national borders—teaches us that we are all vulnerable to the effects of environmental, social, health, and financial problems within nations. The so-called local problems of developing countries, or developed countries for that matter, are often linked to global problems—problems whose resolution is in our common interest and requires the active participation of all members of the international community. While many funders have yet to grapple with this phenomenon—and the small number of foundations actually engaged in international grantmaking reflects that fact—some are responding by extending their domestic areas of interest into the global field or applying lessons learned through domestic programs, such as those on conflict resolution, to situations overseas, and vice versa. A few international funders have adopted grantmaking guidelines that focus on specific issues and problems, rather than on regions. Some are imagining a "third way" of grantmaking—the Ford Foundation calls it "global grantmaking"—that seeks to avoid the domestic-versus-international paradigm and instead attempts to help grantees identify, monitor, and respond to international events and trends that affect local interests (Pasic, 1998). Of course, the blurring of distinctions among global and local issues also contributes to the emergence of new partners and partnerships in international grantmaking, since the need to wed local knowledge with national and international policy acumen becomes steadily more apparent.

Interestingly enough, if the interdependence of nations and peoples can be said to be the defining characteristic of the post–Cold War international scene, it is also emerging as a defining characteristic of post–Cold War international grantmaking. Ostensibly separate issue areas and problems are increasingly perceived to be interrelated; different sectors and disciplines are called upon to collaborate in holistic approaches to problem solving; and the borders that divide grantmaking into domestic and international categories are becoming increasingly permeable.

## *The role of foundations in global problem solving*

International or cross-border grantmaking is not without its technical difficulties for American foundations. Communications and reporting are made more complicated by language differences and differences in the legal and regulatory structures that govern civil society organizations in other countries. For private foundations, which are restricted to grantmaking for "exclusively charitable purposes," there is the challenge of determining—without the benefit of a 501(c)(3) ruling from the IRS—whether or not a potential foreign grantee is the equivalent of a charitable organization in the United States. Several efforts are under way to reduce these obstacles to cross-border grantmaking by identifying best practices, codifying information about nonprofit legislation in countries around the world, and developing standard forms. The Council on Foundations has launched an International Programs Initiative, for example, and the International Center for Not-for-Profit Law in Washington, D.C., is developing a Web site database of laws, regulations, and legal commentaries on the international nonprofit sector.

These difficulties notwithstanding, many observers have lamented the small share of U.S. foundation grantmaking that goes to international programs, especially at a time when globalization so profoundly affects us. World Bank president James Wolfensohn, speaking at the 1998 annual meeting of the Council on Foundations, issued a passionate call for foundations, not to abandon their local concerns, but to consider adding a global dimension or applying a global perspective to their grantmaking as well. "Take a small part of what you're doing, if you're not already doing things internationally, and experiment," he urged. "The responsibilities we have do not end with our cities and communities. They end with a global view. And for those of us who think we can finish our lives thinking only about our local institutions and our local activities, remember that in thirty years' time, when this meeting is held again in Washington, our children are not going to have that luxury." It is a message that will bear frequent repetition in an American political context of weakened commitment to all forms of cooperative international engagement.

But perhaps another kind of appeal can be made as well, by asking whether foundations, given their very nature and by virtue of their special experiences, might have a unique and necessary role to play in effective global problem solving in an interdependent world. The answer, we at the RBF believe, is yes.

In an era of broadened and integrated agendas, foundations' relative "freedom from the crises of transition" enables them to "invest in experiments that connect and reconnect fields of study and spheres of endeavor whose boundaries need to be reconsidered" (Pasic, 1998, p. 17). Working in partnership with NGOs as well as with corporations and government entities, foundations can bring to the international arena their extensive experience in convening discussants, advancing key policy debates, and encouraging dialogue among representatives of different sectors, disciplines, and points of view.

In an era when new, nonstate players are increasingly influential on the international scene, foundation support for civil society organizations takes on crucial significance. The availability of funding, and especially flexible funding, is no small matter. In transitional regions of the world such as South Africa and the formerly Communist countries of Eastern Europe, the premature withdrawal of foreign funding before local sources of support are available could undermine the full reactivation of civil life on which democratization, social stability, and environmentally and culturally sensitive development depend. It is for this reason that the RBF and several other American foundations, including C.S. Mott, Soros, and Ford, have embarked on an unprecedented public-private partnership with USAID to raise bridge funding to help NGOs in fifteen Central and Eastern European countries achieve greater self-reliance and self-sufficiency.

Foundations can also draw on a long history of working with civil society organizations to increase their capacities for collective action, policy analysis, and public outreach. These are capacities NGOs, particularly indigenous NGOs, must have if they are to engage in productive partnerships with agencies and entities that are often much larger and better established than they are.

Finally, in an era when distinctions between domestic and international issues are blurring, another foundation contribution has become absolutely critical: the ability of foundations to help educate the American public and policymakers about the need to invest meaningful resources—money, of course, but also resources of commitment and vision—in cooperative international efforts to solve critical global problems. Foundations and their grantees can help place international issues in a persuasive conceptual framework that provides a compelling rationale for U.S. involvement in global problem solving, and that offers an equally compelling picture of the consequences of failure to engage. Such a framework will also make clear the need for new and reformed institutional arrangements—both public and private—to address global challenges.

This kind of foundation engagement in international issues has the potential to build broader and stronger constituencies for international engagement itself. Such constituencies are vitally important if the NGOs and grassroots groups, government agencies, and multilateral organizations that stand on the front lines of global problem-solving are to garner the support—human, financial, and political—they so urgently need.

### *References*

Pasic, A. *Foundations in Security: An Overview of Foundation Visions, Programs, and Grantees.* New York: Rockefeller Brothers Fund, 1998.

Renz, L., Samson-Atienza, J., Trieber, R. R., and Tran, T. *International Grantmaking: A Report on U.S. Foundation Trends.* New York: Foundation Center in cooperation with Council on Foundations, 1997.

Wolfensohn, J. D. "Remarks at Council of Foundations Luncheon, Apr. 28, 1998." [http://www.worldbank.org/html/extdr/extme/jdwsp042898.htm]. URL active as of April 1999.

COLIN G. CAMPBELL *is president of the Rockefeller Brothers Fund, where he guides a grantmaking program that emphasizes the concept of global interdependence, concentrating on the areas of sustainable resource use and world security. Before joining the Fund in 1988, Campbell spent eighteen years as president of Wesleyan University.*

PRISCILLA LEWIS *is director of communications and special assistant to the president at the Rockefeller Brothers Fund. She was formerly vice president for publications at the Council for Aid to Education and director of publications at the Russell Sage Foundation.*

*If grantmakers and grantseekers can communicate more frequently and more frankly, the organizational changes that take place in foundations in the next century can be productive and rewarding.*

# 7

# Changing perspectives: Evolution not revolution

*Sandra A. Glass*

AS DOROTHY RIDINGS POINTS OUT in the initial chapter, the grantmaking world sees the necessity for greater emphasis on accountability. Whether foundations are regional, community, international, or special purpose, a major part of this accountability can be realized through improved communication—airing policies, demystifying procedures. These are the contributions the authors of this volume have made by describing their organizations' missions, current activities, and especially their anticipated changes.

Other themes link the chapters and illuminate the sometimes arcane foundation goals and grantmaking procedures: To deal with actual growth and to anticipate future growth, foundation boards and staffs are increasingly engaged in long-range planning. As the foundations rethink their programs, they are using experts to assist with setting new directions, and they have recognized the importance of getting to know their constituencies. Many are also including representatives of social and educational agencies on their advisory committees.

NEW DIRECTIONS FOR PHILANTHROPIC FUNDRAISING, NO. 23, SPRING 1999 © JOSSEY-BASS PUBLISHERS

The foundations represented here have stressed cooperation and alliance building as goals for the future. While McIlnay's recent study emphasizes the problems of building trust and partnerships between grantmakers and grantseekers because of their unequal stature (1997, pp. 150–169), the chapters in this volume refute that assertion. The authors believe that the realization that partners *can* solve problems will be the prevalent view in the coming century. Publication of news of successful projects developed cooperatively by foundations and one or more agencies will encourage other grantmakers to follow these models.

## *Changes within foundations*

Rather than maintaining that foundations will suddenly reach the twenty-first century and radically reform themselves, it is much more accurate to understand that they are involved in a rather steady process of evolution. Moreover, several of these gradual changes can have a significant impact on grantseeking.

### *New professional staff*

The growth of foundations will necessitate increased numbers of staff members, and fortunately many of them will come from nonprofit agencies. They will be able to empathize with grant applicants and will also have high standards as they assess proposals. They may, however, also continue the trend toward developing foundation-initiated programs rather than responding to priorities of applicant organizations that need help with capital construction or operating support.

This emphasis on staff-developed programs is not, as grantseekers sometimes believe, an arbitrary effort at self-aggrandizement. Most foundation staff members have heeded Robert Payton's well-stated advice to "live for philanthropy" rather than to "live on philanthropy" (1988, pp. 71–88). They want to help society and to make effective grants. These program officers, especially new staff, are constantly looking for ways to fulfill the expectations of their bosses—the foundations' CEOs and board members. Merely assessing proposals that come in over the transom is not as creative as designing new ways to reform communities, regions, or nations. Thus they receive credit and appreciation for proactive grantmaking, and support for specifically designed foundation projects will probably continue, or even increase, in the future.

### *New technologies*

More and more foundations are realizing the advantages of new technologies. Many will, for example, respond to queries by e-mail, and some will review proposal drafts submitted by fax or e-mail. A small number will even accept electronically submitted proposals, and that number may grow as they follow the example of federal agencies.

Grantseekers are finding that foundation Web sites—kept up to date with information about guidelines, new programs, and recent grants—are becoming their most important sources of information. Each month additional foundations are establishing sites, and foundation leaders are encouraging and helping smaller foundations to employ this technology. Within the next decade it should be easy to obtain current and accurate information about most of the country's major grantmaking organizations.

### *Young grantmakers*

Much has been written recently in the popular press about the new generation of affluent Americans, who are younger, busier, and less knowledgeable about philanthropy than the traditional older givers (for example, Sloan, 1997, pp. 48–55; and "Philanthropy in America," 1998, pp. 19-21). Whether their wealth comes from technology, entertainment, athletics, or bequests, many of these potential new donors are beginning to consider establishing foundations.

As these new philanthropists become more active, certain changes should be noted by grantseekers: Grants may go to the types of organizations that have influenced the young people in their formative years or those that are capturing their attention, and these may *not* be traditional higher education institutions or national social agencies. If they have young children, precollegiate education may be a priority for giving, as may be the environment or issues in their local urban communities.

Busy young grantmakers may hire staff to deal with the public, but it is equally likely that they may make changes in the proposal process. Rather than reading long proposals with many appendices describing elaborate projects, the new foundation leaders may insist upon brief outlines accompanied by detailed project budgets. These grantmakers may also want to reduce proposal assessment time. Foundation fundraisers may, therefore, have to revise their concept of the ideal proposal in the coming years.

## *Evolution in fundraising*

As changes take place within foundations, it becomes imperative that fundraisers take the opportunity to reassess their methods. This does not mean abandoning high professional standards of cultivation and proposal presentation. Proposals that make a case for both excellence and need and that present a project to a foundation in a formal manner will continue to generate grants. There will be, however, new techniques for fundraisers to heed. It is not possible to anticipate what many of these will be as foundations evolve, but some of the following may emerge:

- Sophisticated foundation staff members will be interested in the long-range planning capabilities and positive fiscal profiles of applicant agencies. The business expertise and financial dimensions of proposals will become more important.
- Foundations may become increasingly interested in multi-institutional projects. As cooperation becomes more popular among foundations, or among foundations and government agencies, these grantmakers will also encourage applicants to form coalitions in their cities and regions. Because multiagency programs take longer to plan and develop, fundraisers will need to allow more lead time from inception of an idea to receipt of a grant.

• Applicants will have to develop new ways to communicate concisely with foundations. Busy staff members, trained in the electronic age, may not have the time or the desire to read traditional newsletters or alumni magazines. Nor will they want to spend hours watching videotapes from applicants. Perhaps the new method will be for agencies to have their own Web sites, organized so that foundation program officers can get all the information from an informative and attractive "fact page."

• If foundation-initiated programs become too specific, grantseekers will need to learn how to say "no, thank you" to offers of funding that do not meet their priority needs.

Only rarely have agencies been willing to turn down foundation support, and little has been written about the importance of communicating frankly with grantmakers. Deborah Callard broaches the issue by questioning whether an institution will endanger its long-term relationship with a foundation if it declines a request to submit an invited proposal (1989, p. 122). The new millennium does seem to be an appropriate time for professional and successful fundraisers to become bold enough to explain to foundations that an unreasonable challenge grant or a nonessential bell tower might not be the best use of funds for all parties involved. Declining an opportunity to submit a proposal might jeopardize one grant, but it can engender longer-term respect. Through these exchanges, foundations will learn skills from grantseekers on how better to set priorities for giving.

This is indeed a restatement of the theme of communication that runs though this volume. The more interchange of ideas, plans, and visions that can be shared among foundations and applicants, the better will be the outlook for foundation philanthropy in the future.

### *References*

Callard, D. "Positioning the Private Research University for Foundation Grants." In M. K. Murphy (ed.), *Cultivating Foundation Support for Education.* Washington, D.C.: Council for Advancement and Support of Education, 1989.

McIlnay, D. P. *How Foundations Work.* San Francisco: Jossey-Bass, 1997.

Payton, R. L. *Philanthropy: Voluntary Action for the Public Good.* Phoenix: Oryx Press, 1988.

"Philanthropy in America." *Economist*, May 30, 1998, pp. 19–21.
Sloan, A. "The New Rich." *Newsweek*, Aug. 4, 1997, pp. 48–55.

SANDRA A. GLASS *is an independent consultant for education and philanthropy. She is program vice president emerita of the W. M. Keck Foundation, where she supervised higher education programs in science, engineering, and liberal arts for sixteen years. She also worked in development and administration for ten years at the Claremont Colleges.*

# Index

Academic institutions. *See* Higher education
Academics, support for, 59–61, 63–65
Accountability: and disclosure provisions, 14n.3; greater emphasis on, 8–9, 44, 85; and measurability of outcomes, 15; and peer review, 21–22, 55
Advice and counsel for institution-wide projects, 55
Advisory committees, 85
Advocacy by foundations: right to, 13; and targeted grantmaking, 7–8, 21–22, 45–46
Affinity groups, professional, 8
Age groups of philanthropists, 7–8, 11, 87–88. *See also* Groups, beneficiary
Alaskans, studying needs of, 34
Alliances. *See* Public-private alliances
Architects, 19–20
Areas, program. *See* Program areas, philanthropic
Assessment of proposals: and pairing applicants, 36–37; quicker, 88
Asset levels: community foundation, 44–45; growth of foundation, 7, 14n.2, 41, 71; and regionalism, 30–31
Associations of grantmakers, 12. *See also* Council on Foundations
Atlanta, the Community Foundation for Greater, 47–48, 49

Baby-boom generation as philanthropists, 7–8, 11, 87–88
Board leaders, 14n.3, 44
Bridge funding for NGOs abroad, 82–83
Building codes, philanthropic support for advanced, 20

Callard, D., 89
Camille and Henry Dreyfus Foundation, 53
Capital, danger in international flow of, 74
Capital campaign, 63–64
Career development, funding of, 59–60, 63
Carleton College, 53
Change, of energy use in buildings, 19–20; security and peaceful, 74. *See also* Theory of change
Changes within foundations, 86–89; new technologies, 87; in professional staff roles, 86–87
Charitable organizations, 16, 44; accountability of, 9; foreign grantee, 81. *See also specific organization names*
Charity versus philanthropy, 16
Chernow, R., 16, 17
Civil society organizations, international support for, 82–83
Cold War, new challenges after the, 74
College catalogues, mission statements from, 53
Columbus Foundation, 43
Commercial donor-directed funds, 9–10, 14n.3
Communication by foundations: around the world, 81; with external audiences, 13, 87. *See also* Grantmakers and grantseekers
Community, the international. *See* Globalization; International grantmaking from the United States
Community enrichment, foundation-sponsored, 39–40, 82–83

Community Foundation for Greater Atlanta, Inc., 47–48, 49
Community foundations, 28, 43–50; competitiveness of, 9–10; connecting donors and communities, 46–47; donor services by, 47–48; features common to, 44; regional thinking by, 48–49; types of funds in, 44–46. *See also* regional foundations
Competition: for-profit sector, 48; nonprofit sector, 9–10
Conferences, professional, 8, 12
Conflict resolution, grantmaking for, 73, 77
Connections and cooperation: foundations as enabling grantee, 36, 40, 46–47, 50, 56–57; for global problem solving, 81–83. *See also* Public-private alliances
Constituencies, getting to know, 31, 33–34, 37–38, 48–49, 85
Corporate philanthropy: commercial donor-directed funds, 9–10; foundations, 28; regulation of, 10, 14n.3
Council on Foundations, 5–6, 14; conferences, 8, 12; international initiatives, 81; and professionalization, 8; survey research findings, 12–13
Cross-border grantmaking, 80, 81–83; technical obstacles to, 81
Cross-cultural studies, support planning for, 60–61
Cross-sectoral partnership, 79–80
Customer service, expanding, 47, 48

David and Lucile Packard Foundation, 14n.2
Decision making: change and energy use, 19–20; focused philanthropic, 16–17; about philanthropic regionalism, 31
Democracy: education in a, 53; global conditions for, 76, 82
Designated funds, 46
Developers, building, 19–20
Development: community, 39–40, 46–47, 82–83; faculty, 60–61, 63; international, 78, 79
Devolution, demand due to, 69
Diversity and inclusiveness of grantmaking, 11–12, 74
Donor-directed and donor-advised funds, 45; regulation of, 10, 14n.3
Donors: connecting communities and, 46–47; customer services for, 47, 48; hands-on style, 8, 47–48; rise in younger, 7–8, 11, 50, 87–88

Educational roles of foundations, 39–40, 53–54, 58; building constituencies for global problem solving, 76, 77, 83
Energy Foundation, 18–20, 26
Enrichment programs, foundation-sponsored, 39–40, 56
Environment and habitat, 37–38; energy use in the built, 19–20
Ethnic divisions, post– Cold War, 74
Experts, roles of, 17, 33–34, 55, 85
External review. *See* Peer review; Proposals
Exxon Education Foundation, 59

Faculty: development grants, 60–61, 63; proposal preparation skills, 59–60, 65
Federal agencies. *See* Public-private alliances
Federal agency missions, 54, 82
Field travel, staff, 33, 35
Field-building grants, 23, 24–25
Field-of-interest funds, 45
Focused philanthropy, 15–26; areas of, 15–16, 72; clear goals for, 17–18; and follow-through, 24; funding scale of, 22–23; for global problem solving, 81–83; and grantseekers, 24–26; long-term commitment to, 23–24; and peer review, 21–22, 25; Rockefeller legacy of, 16–17; studying other efforts in, 20; theory of change basis of, 18–21; using expert opinion, 17, 33–34. *See also* Groups, beneficiary
Ford Foundation, 80, 82
Foundation Center study of international grantmaking, 70–71

Foundation-initiated programs: declining to submit proposals for, 89; trend toward developing, 86–87
Foundations: changes in, 86–89; demystifying, 1; diversity of, 58; future of, 50, 65–66; global problem-solving roles of, 81–83; identifying potential partner, 57–58, 64; interactive, 32–34, 36–37; mission statements of, 53–54; number of U.S., 1, 30, 71; proactive or reactive, 32; sources of information on, 13; three grantmaking styles of, 32; types and percentages of, 28–29. *See also* Staff, foundation
Fulbright Scholars Program, 61
Fund for the Improvement of Postsecondary Education (FIPSE), 56, 64
Funding: bridge, 82–83; commercial donor-directed, 9–10, 14n.3; of grassroots organizations abroad, 72, 76, 82. *See also* Groups, beneficiary; Program areas, philanthropic
Fundraising: development seminars to aid, 39; evolution in, 88–89
Future: of foundations, 50; of public-private alliances, 65–66, 81–83

Gates, F. T., 16
Geographical areas. *See* International grantmaking from the United States; Regional foundations
Giamatti, A. B., 66
Gillmor, P., 14n.3
Global Interdependence Initiative (RBF), 76
Global Security grantmaking guidelines, RBF, 74
Globalization: challenges, 74, 77; and cooperative problem solving, 80, 81–83; and global or local problems, 77, 80; of philanthropy, 11–12. *See also* International grantmaking from the United States
Goals of philanthropy: and follow-through, 24, 82; long-term commitment to, 23–24, 85; writing focused, 17–18
Grant recipients: communication by, 33, 89; reporting of, 14n.3
Grantmakers and grantseekers: connecting community, 46–47; cooperation between, 86; frank communication between, 89; interactive relationship of, 32, 33–34, 36–37; meetings at the foundation, 33; and peer review, 21–22, 25, 55–56, 65; theory of change understanding between, 24–25. *See also* Philanthropists
Grantmaking: proactive, 86–87; third way of, 80; three styles of, 32
Grants: declining of, 89; factors in determining types of, 31, 58
Grassroots organizations abroad, funding of, 72, 76
Groups, beneficiary, 11; Alaskans, 34; convening and matchmaking of, 36, 40; funding for special, 7–8, 45, 72, 78; interorganizational, 36; overseas grassroots and indigenous, 71–72, 76; of regional foundations, 33–34, 36; Youth Workers Round Tables, 39–40. *See also* Focused philanthropy
Groups in philanthropy: foreign grantmaking associations, 12; professional affinity, 8

Health and safety, 16–17, 77
Higher education: faculty development grants, 60–61, 63; faculty proposal skills, 59–60, 65; future support for, 65–66; research support, 34–35, 38. *See also* Public-private alliances
Howard Hughes Medical Institute (HHMI), 56, 64
Human rights agenda and grantmaking, 78
Human security, and international grantmaking, 73–77
Humanities grantmaking, 54, 61, 64

Independent and regional foundations, 29
Institutional change, using itineraries for, 62–65
Institutional missions, 52–53

Interactive foundations, 32–34, 36–37
Interdependence of nations and peoples, 73–77, 80, 81–83
Intermediary institutions, philanthropy through, 16–17
Internal Revenue Service (IRS). *See* Tax provisions
International Center for Not-for-Profit Law, 81
International grantmaking from the United States, 11–12, 69–83; challenges for, 77–80; and global problem solving, 81–83; holistic versus categorized, 80; for international affairs, 72–73; overview of, 70–73; statistics on, 71; trends in security-related, 73–77
International Programs Initiative, 81
International studies, support planning for, 60–61
Interviews, Council on Foundations survey, 12
Itineraries: designing strategic, 57–59, 62–63; scenarios illustrating, 59–61, 63–65

John D. and Catherine T. MacArthur Foundation, 18, 79
Joyce Mertz-Gilmore Foundation, 18, 79

Landlords and tenants, building, 20
Laws and regulations: international nonprofit sector, 81; proposed, 14n.3; taxation, 10, 14n.1
Leadership program, youth workers, 39
Letter of declination, benefit of, 56

M. J. Murdock Charitable Trust, 27–41; asset levels, 30–31; challenges of being regional, 32–36; description of, 30; enrichment or value-added programs, 39–40, 56; opportunities in being regional, 32–36; and Pacific Northwest issues, 37–38
Matching funds, institutional, 65
Matchmaking, foundation-assisted. *See* Meetings
McIlnay, D. P., 86
Medical research philanthropy, 16–17
Meetings: of grantees for making connections, 36, 40, 46–47, 56–57; invitational grantmaker-grantseeker, 33; with visiting scholars, 33–34
Merrill Lynch & Company, 48
Mission statements: educational institution, 52–53; federal agency, 54; foundation, 53–54
Multinational philanthropy. *See* International grantmaking from the United States
Multistate grantmakers. *See* Regional foundations
Murdock Trust. *See* M. J. Murdock Charitable Trust

National Endowment for the Humanities (NEH), 61; Focus Grant Program, 64
National Foundation on the Arts and the Humanities, 54
National governments and nonstate actors, 76, 79
National Science Foundation (NSF), 54, 56; Faculty Early Career Development Program, 60, 63; program aims statement from, 63
New York Community Trust, 43
Nongovernmental organizations (NGOs), 75–76, 79; public-private international support for, 82–83
Nonprofit sector: competition, 9–10; foundations and the, 13, 46–47; the international, 81–83; and national governments, 76, 79
Number of foundations. *See* Statistics

Operating foundations, 29
Ortega y Gasset, J., 51, 52
Overseas recipients. *See* International grantmaking from the United States

Pacific Northwest common-thread issues, 37–38
Partnerships: cross-sectoral international, 79–80, 81–83; focusing on goal of, 62; between grantmakers and grantseekers, 86; and grant-

making scale, 22–23; making connections for, 46–47, 50. *See also* Public-private alliances
Pasic, A., 73, 80, 82
Payton, R. L., 86
Peace and security, funding for, 72–73
Peer review, 21–22, 25, 55–56, 65
People: board leaders, 14n.3, 44; dealing with, 59; studying building industry, 19–20; worldwide human security of, 73–77, 78. *See also* Groups, beneficiary; Meetings; Staff, foundation
Pew Charitable Trusts, 18
Philanthropists: attitudes of younger, 7–8, 50, 87–88; intergenerational wealth among, 7, 11; the new hands-on, 8, 47–48
Philanthropy, organized: and American higher education, 66; changes in categories of, 80; focused scale of, 22–23; growth of, 6–7; holistic versus categorized, 80; international, 11–12, 69–83; major trends in, 6–12; versus charity, 16
Pifer, A., 58
Planning, long-range, 23–24, 85
Ploughshares Fund, 23–24
Population groups. *See* Groups, beneficiary
Proactive grantmaking, 86–87
Professionalization of philanthropy, 8, 12
Program areas, philanthropic: broadening and integration of, 77–79; development-related international, 78, 79; focused, 15–16, 72. *See also* Focused philanthropy; Groups, beneficiary
Program directors, expertise of, 33–34
Programmatic development grants to educational institutions, 60–61
Proposals: business and financial sophistication of, 88; change strategy importance in, 19–21, 25; declining to submit, 89; electronic submission of, 87; evaluation of, 21, 34–35; external review of, 56; institutional internal budget, 64–65; mission and goals in, 52; multi-institutional project, 88; planning for writing, 59–60; questions to be addressed by, 55–57; shorter, 88
Public and foundation relationships, 44; and accessibility, 49; building constituencies for global problem solving, 76, 77, 83; opinion survey, 13
Public charity status, 44, 81
Public-private alliances, 51–66; the benefits of, 55–57; and federal agency missions, 54; focusing on goal of, 62; and foundation missions, 53–54; future of, 65–66; and institutional missions, 51–53; international, 81–83; as investments, 57; multidimensional complexity of, 58; multiple routes for, 62–63; sample itinerary scenarios, 59–61, 63–65; strategic itinerary plan for, 57–59; supporting indigenous NGOs abroad, 82–83; with USAID, 82. *See also* Partnerships

Questions: accountability, 65; about future public-private alliances, 65–66; from potential funding partners, 57–58; for scholarly proposals to answer, 55, 56

RBF. *See* Rockefeller Brothers Fund
Reddy, A., 20–21
Region, knowing the, 31, 37–38; community foundations and, 47, 48–49
Regional foundations, 27–41; advantages and opportunities of, 36–37; and asset levels, 30–31; challenges for, 32–36; defining, 27–28, 29; and grantmaking interests, 31; grantmaking styles of, 32; interactivity of, 32–34, 36–37; and the Pacific Northwest, 37–38; studies by, 34; trends and emphases of, 40–41; types of, 28–29. *See also* Community foundations
Renz, L., 70
Research: building industry, 19–20; on foundations, 7, 12–13, 43; medical, 16–17; scientific, 34–35, 38, 64. *See also* Statistics

Research Corporation of Tucson, Arizona, 35
Rockefeller, J. D., Sr., 16
Rockefeller Brothers Fund (RBF), 82; security-related grantmaking, 73–77, 79
Rockefeller Foundation, 18, 79; focused philanthropy principles of the, 16–17; Web site address, 26
Rural health care, 38

Sabbatical applications, academic, 64
Scale of philanthropy. *See* Focused philanthropy; International grantmaking from the United States; Regional foundations
Scholars, visiting, 33–34
Scholarship and teaching, 59–60. *See also* Higher education
Scientific research, support of, 34–35, 38, 64
Security-related grantmaking, trends in, 73–77
Seminars, development, 39
Skidmore College, 53
Sloan, A., 87
Social change strategy. *See* Theory of change
Solar Development Corporation, worldwide, 79
Special-purpose philanthropy. *See* Focused philanthropy; Groups, beneficiary
Staff, foundation: advice and counsel by, 55, 59; regional program director, 33–34, 35; support, 35, 40
Statewide foundations, 44
Statistics: on community foundations, 43; on creation of foundations, 7; on international grantmaking, 71; on number of U.S. foundations, 1, 30, 71; on percentages of types of foundations, 28–29. *See also* Research
Study-abroad program, support planning for, 60–61
Support staff. *See* Staff, foundation
Survey research: on community foundations, 43; Council on Foundations, 12–13

Targeted grantmaking, 7–8, 45–46; and peer review, 21–22
Tax provisions, 10, 13; and disclosure, 14n.3; for gifts of appreciated property, 6–7; public charity status, 44, 81
Teaching and scholarship, 59–60
Technologies: new, 87; studying building industry performance and, 19–20
Territory. *See* Regional foundations
Theory of change: as basis of strategy, 18–19; defining steps to success, 20–21; elements of a, 19–21; use by grantseekers, 24–26
"Third way" of grantmaking, 80
Touchpoint opportunities, 47
Travel, staff field, 33, 35

Universidad Metropolitana, 53
Unrestricted funds, 45
U.S. government: domestic and foreign policies, 77, 82; federal agency missions, 54, 82; NEH, 61, 64; NSF, 54, 56, 60, 63; USAID, 82. *See also* Tax provisions

Value-added or enrichment programs, foundation-sponsored, 39–40, 56
Volunteer board involvement, 14n.3

W. M. Keck Foundation, 53–54
Weapons of mass destruction, reducing threat of, 23–24
Web sites: applicant agency, 89; foundation, 87; Global Security grantmaking guidelines (RBF), 74; on international nonprofit sector laws, 81
Wolfensohn, J. D., 81
Women. *See* Groups, beneficiary
World Bank, 79
World War II generation, 11
Writing: focused philanthropy goals, 17–18; proposals, 52, 55–57, 59–60, 65, 88

Youth Workers Round Tables, 39–40

# Back Issue/Subscription Order Form

Copy or detach and send to:
**Jossey-Bass Inc., Publishers, 350 Sansome Street, San Francisco, CA 94104-1342**

Call or fax toll free!
**Phone 888-378-2537 6AM-5PM PST; Fax 800-605-2665**

Back issues: Please send me the following issues at $25 each
(Important: please include series initials and issue number, such as PF10)

1. PF ______________________________

______________________________

______________________________

$ __________ Total for single issues

$ __________ Shipping charges (for single issues ***only;*** subscriptions are exempt from shipping charges): Up to $30, add $5⁵⁰ • $30⁰¹–$50, add $6⁵⁰ $50⁰¹–$75, add $7⁵⁰ • $75⁰¹–$100, add $9 • $100⁰¹–$150, add $10 Over $150, call for shipping charge

Subscriptions Please ❑ start ❑ renew my subscription to *New Directions for Philanthropic Fundraising* for the year 1999 at the following rate:

❑ Individual $67 ❑ Institutional $115

**NOTE:** Subscriptions are quarterly, and are for the calendar year only. Subscriptions begin with the spring issue of the year indicated above. For shipping outside the U.S., please add $25.

$ __________ Total single issues and subscriptions (CA, IN, NJ, NY and DC residents, add sales tax for single issues. NY and DC residents must include shipping charges when calculating sales tax. NY and Canadian residents only, add sales tax for subscriptions)

❑ Payment enclosed (U.S. check or money order only)

❑ VISA, MC, AmEx, Discover Card #__________________ Exp. date________

Signature ________________________ Day phone ______________

❑ Bill me (U.S. institutional orders only. Purchase order required)

Purchase order #______________________________

Name ______________________________

Address ______________________________

______________________________

______________________________

Phone____________________ E-mail ______________

For more information about Jossey-Bass Publishers, visit our Web site at:
www.josseybass.com **PRIORITY CODE = ND1**

# Previous Issues Available

NEW DIRECTIONS FOR PHILANTHROPIC FUNDRAISING

PF22 Understanding and Improving the Language of Fundraising, *Timothy L. Seiler*

PF21 Capital Campaigns: Realizing Their Power and Potential, *Andrea Kihlstedt, Robert Pierpont*

PF20 Small Nonprofits: Strategies for Fundraising Success, *Mary Louise Mussoline*

PF19 Women as Fundraisers: Their Experience in and Influence on an Emerging Profession, *Julie C. Conry*

PF18 Marketing the Nonprofit: The Challenge of Fundraising in a Consumer Culture, *Margaret M. Maxwell*

PF17 The Practice of Stewardship in Religious Fundraising, *Daniel Conway, Cecelia Hart Price*

PF16 Developing Major Gifts, *Dwight F. Burlingame, James M. Hodge*

PF15 The Professionalization of Fundraising: Implications for Education, Practice, and Accountability, *Eugene R. Tempel, Sara B. Cobb, Warren F. Ilchman*

PF14 Building and Managing an Asset Base: Information and Advice for Nonprofit Organizations, *Jimmie A. Alford*

PF13 What Fundraisers Need to Know About State and Federal Regulation: How It Can Influence All Aspects of Their Work, *Rita A. Fuerst*

PF12 Alternative Revenue Sources: Prospects, Requirements, and Concerns for Nonprofits, *Dwight F. Burlingame, Warren F. Ilchman*

PF11 Improving Fundraising with Technology, *James D. Miller, Deborah Strauss*

PF10 Communicating Effectively with Major Donors, *Dianne A. Brehmer*

PF9 Fundraising by Public Institutions, *Thomas H. Jeavons*

PF8 Cultures of Giving II: How Heritage, Gender, Wealth, and Values Influence Philanthropy, *Charles H. Hamilton, Warren F. Ilchman*

PF6 Ethics in Fundraising: Putting Values into Practice, *Marianne G. Briscoe*

PF5 Nonprofit Organizational Culture: What Fundraisers Need to Know, *Royster C. Hedgepeth*

PF4 Achieving Trustee Involvement in Fundraising, *Timothy L. Seiler, Kay Sprinkel Grace*

PF3 Financial Practices for Effective Fundraising, *James M. Greenfield*

PF2 Women as Donors, Women as Philanthropists, *Abbie J. von Schlegell, Joan M. Fisher*

PF1 Fundraising Matters: True Stories of How Raising Funds Fulfills Dreams, *Michael Seltzer*